Dying for a Drink

PATRICK BRODE

DYING FOR A DRINK

How a Prohibition Preacher Got Away with Murder

BIBLIOASIS
WINDSOR, ONTARIO

THE ONTARIO HISTORICAL SOCIETY

FIRST EDITION

Library and Archives Canada Cataloguing in Publication

Brode, Patrick, 1950-, author
   Dying for a drink : how a prohibition preacher got away with murder / Patrick Brode.

ISBN 978-1-77196-268-1 (softcover).—ISBN 978-1-77196-297-1

       1. Trumble, Beverly--Death and burial. 2. Spracklin, Joseph Oswald Leslie, 1886-. 3. Prohibition--Ontario--Windsor. 4. Temperance--Ontario--Windsor. 5. Murder--Ontario--Windsor. I. Title.

HV5091.C3B76 2018   364.1'3320971332   C2018-901746-5

Edited by Sharon Hanna
Copy-edited by James Grainger
Typeset and designed by Chris Andrechek

Published with the generous assistance of the Canada Council for the Arts, which last year invested $153 million to bring the arts to Canadians throughout the country, and the financial support of the Government of Canada. Biblioasis also acknowledges the support of the Ontario Arts Council (OAC), an agency of the Government of Ontario, which last year funded 1,709 individual artists and 1,078 organizations in 204 communities across Ontario, for a total of $52.1 million, and the contribution of the Government of Ontario through the Ontario Book Publishing Tax Credit and the Ontario Media Development Corporation.

PRINTED AND BOUND IN CANADA

Contents

INTRODUCTION

On November 6, 1920, two men confronted each other in an armed standoff in the town of Sandwich, Ontario. One of them would die.

Beverley "Babe" Trumble, one of the combatants, was a rough and tumble tavern keeper. He was known to sell liquor and beer to Americans in his popular roadhouse, the Chappell House. The man challenging Trumble that evening was an enforcer acting on behalf of the provincial government. But not only was he a licensed officer of the law, he was an ordained minister of the Methodist Church of Canada. The Reverend J.O.L. Spracklin was already something of a legendary figure across Ontario for his no-holds barred approach to imposing the temperance laws. Disdaining any need for search warrants or other legal niceties, Spracklin and his special agents had been bursting into liquor dens and administering their own personal brand of justice to those who defied the morality laws. On the evening of November 6, Spracklin and his men had broken into the Chappell House in search of contraband liquor.

Trumble, an individual who stood by his rights, was determined to resist them.

This confrontation, which must have lasted only a few seconds, was in many ways the high-water mark of the temperance movement that had been such a powerful political force in Ontario for decades. It was a collision between evangelical Ontario, which considered the consumption of alcohol to be an unforgiveable evil, and a modern society that welcomed a more liberal lifestyle. For moral purists such as the Reverend Spracklin, drinking was a vile habit that robbed men of their free will and diverted them from their responsibilities to their families. On the receiving end of Spracklin's fire was a roadhouse operator who represented what the province was becoming: a consumer-oriented, leisure-seeking culture that defied Victorian mores. The Jazz Age was about to explode, and it would resist attempts to rein in its exuberance. Some entrepreneurs were determined to meet the needs of this emerging materialistic society and profit by it. Babe Trumble was one of these visionaries, and it was his misfortune to cross paths with one of the most zealous defenders of the old ways.

Significantly, this confrontation took place on the Detroit River border, in a transnational area that was neither entirely Canadian nor American. With a diverse population that came from more metropolitan parts of Europe, and with a significant non-Protestant element, the Windsor border area (usually referred to as the "Border Cities") did not conform to the expectations of the rest of the province. Moreover, the inhabitants looked to the adjacent American metropolis of Detroit for the lead on cultural and social affairs rather than to the distant provincial capital of Toronto. Early on, the Toronto press grasped that the Detroit River border was different, and they reported on developments on this "frontier" almost as if they were reporting on events in a foreign country. Their readers thrilled to accounts of heavily armed gangs fighting it out for liquor caches secreted in Essex County hideaways. Toronto reporters described how rumrunners who had lived their lives along the shoals and backwaters of the Detroit River braved the enforcers of American Prohibition to run shipments across the international border. Those who lived at a safe distance from these events were either entertained or appalled by the lawlessness along the western border.

In the eyes of some, particularly those in the evangelical movement who had struggled through their lives to foster a temperate, alcohol-free Ontario, something had to be done to bring this unruly region to heel. After decades of struggle and numerous referenda, the movement had finally prevailed in the *Ontario Temperance Act* of 1916. The saloons were closed, and the sale of liquor and beer made a thing of the past. The movement to abolish the bar had the support of the Ontario public, and now it had the force of law. With the appointment of the Reverend J.O.L. Spracklin as a Provincial Inspector in July 1920, the new law found a determined enforcer.

Yet, Spracklin's appointment, and his three tumultuous months in office, would cast doubt on the wisdom of the government imposing goodness and temperance through force of arms. The attempt to impose Victorian controls by a militant clergyman would cause many to question whether religious beliefs had any place in Canadian legal codes. That this militancy could cost a man his life was proof that the crusade for moral reform had gone too far.

1

A TEMPERATE
PROVINCE

The events leading up to the confrontation between Spracklin and Trumble were part of the history of moral reform in Ontario, a long and complicated story with its roots in the human craving for alcohol.

Drinking was a way of life on the early Canadian frontier. Historian Fred Landon concluded that "during its first fifty years as a province, Upper Canada, (later Ontario) must have been one of the least temperate countries in the world. Distilleries and breweries were proportionately as the gasoline stations of a more modern era and a cheap, bad whisky was everywhere available." Whisky, not low-alcohol beer, fueled frontier society. Patrick Shirreff, a Scottish traveler to Upper Canada in the 1830s was shocked at the prevalence of drunkenness, and that so many of his travelling companions were tipsy. Far more than long-settled Scotland, the Canadian frontier was dependent upon hard liquor. Taverns lined most thoroughfares and imbibers considered liquor a protection against impure water. At planting or harvest time, "buckets of whisky went round among fieldhands and regular doses of grog warmed soldiers and sailors on duty... Liquor was quite simply a dietary staple." Social gatherings such as barn raisings were fuelled by the free dispensation of liquor, and the wise builder kept back the offerings until the greater part of the structure was in place. In lieu of currency, liquor was often seen as a commodity, and after a harvest, a farmer could exchange grain for alcohol. Whisky would be served as a common household beverage and children would get used to its taste from infancy. It was apparent that "During the pioneer period the constant consumption of alcoholic stimulants was widespread among all classes of inhabitants. Some of the clergy partook too freely of the beverage, and set an example which others were not slow to follow."[1]

Not everyone condoned this unfettered access to and abuse of alcohol. Public drunkenness was condemned by the province's judges, and in 1835, Judge R.B. Sullivan urged "an inquiry into the cause of the prevalence of intemperance in our city (Toronto)... the greater part of the crimes complained of have originated in drunkenness." Addressing a Sarnia grand jury in 1861, Judge Hagarty noted that this problem was not confined to one area of the province, but rather that "ready access to the 'roadside groggery' was the cause of much of the violence" that plagued rural areas. While it is difficult to calculate the amount of liquor consumed in the early nineteenth century, anecdotal evidence would indicate that it was excessive. The English gentle lady, Anna Jamieson, on her tour of the province in 1833, recorded that in the space from Hamilton to York (Toronto), a distance of forty miles, there were twenty taverns. Added to this were the numbers of "grocery stores" which doubled as drinking spots.

The prevalence of heavy drinking generated a moral backlash. A temperance movement, largely inspired by American revivalists, spread through many parts of Canada. American temperance gained significant momentum after the War of 1812, and by 1835, it had about a million supporters. This movement to control or reduce the level of drinking was part of a wider effort aimed at improving society by abolishing slavery, reforming the justice system, and creating a sober and productive people. Protestant reformism was based on the conviction that social maladies could be solved by government direction. Above all, it was the Methodist Episcopal Church that set the pace of the temperance movement. While the spread of temperance in Canada was not as fast as in the United States, the urge to reform had made itself felt by the mid-1800s. A Toronto rally in 1853 closer to a religious revival than a political meeting called for the suppression of all distilleries and taverns. In 1860, the provincial legislature passed "An Act to diminish the number of licenses issued for the sale of Intoxicating Liquors by Retail" which delegated the role of moral arbiter to the local municipalities. Thanks to the *Canada Temperance Act* (usually called the *Scott Act* after its sponsor, R.W. Scott) of 1878, a local option to prohibit liquor in a county was made available. Municipalities could vote to abolish the sale of liquor and temperance advocates presumed they would leap at the chance. Some did, but in others a self-indulgent majority kept the saloons in business. The end result was a patchwork in which many areas of rural Ontario effectively prohibited taverns and liquor shops. Even in areas that remained wet, legal access to drink was becoming increasingly difficult. The 4,794 tavern licenses issued in 1875 had been reduced to 2,516 in 1905 and to 1,371 by 1914.[2]

In the context of its times, there was little doubt that the temperance movement was a reaction to a genuine problem. The hard drinking of the early 1800s left broken families, lost lives, and abandoned children in its wake. After 1850, many evangelical preachers passionately articulated the case against alcohol. The government had an obligation to protect its people; to intervene to protect them against those who would poison and destroy them. State intervention to prevent the manufacture and sale of alcohol would

Taking a beer break, circa 1899.

be a liberating movement, for Prohibition would finally enable individuals to be truly free, to be rid of the demon that robbed them of their self-control. A series of powerful Methodist preachers including William McKay, Alexander Sutherland, and Robert Wallace preached to Ontarians about the collective need to end the scourge of drinking. Those who sold alcohol were especially blame-worthy for, as the Reverend McKay explained, they created "the woe that is poured into the hearts and homes of our people…"

The middle-class ladies who made up the core of the Women's Christian Temperance Union also advanced the view that abstinence from alcohol was not only a lofty ideal, but a pressing political objective. For the first time, women played a major role in a great international cause. The WCTU would be in the energetic forefront to ban the bar and reinforce the family. Over the later nineteenth century, the temperance movement (by 1874, led by the umbrella group the Dominion Alliance for the Total Suppression of the Liquor Traffic, or simply the "Dominion Alliance") would evolve from a religious movement to a political force to compel the state to prohibit the manufacture and sale of alcohol.[3]

This increased level of agitation was in the face of declining levels of alcohol consumption across Canada. With the frontier days long over, the level of whiskey and wine drinking declined steadily in the late 1800s. While beer consumption rose slightly, this reflected the growing urbanization of the country and the working man's preference for a cheap, low-alcohol beverage. This had the effect of concentrating middle-class concern

Meeting of the Women's Christian Temperance Union in Toronto, 1899.

on the saloon, the preferred venue for working class imbibing. It was the saloon, frequently an insalubrious place where cigar smoke and spilt beer were the primary smells, that revolted the sensibilities of the better classes. According to temperance tracts, the saloon sucked the meager finances from families and created havoc among the poor. It was the duty of the government to close them down.

The national plebiscite on prohibition in 1898 highlighted the gains the temperance movement had made. A majority of voting (male) Canadians voted in favour of national prohibition. However, the Laurier government noted that the majority was thin, the voter turnout small, and significant parts of the country were clearly opposed. Almost all cities voted to remain "wet" and Quebec was entirely hostile to the idea. As a result, the federal government would take no action, and it was apparent that in Canada, the temperance war would have to be waged within the provinces. While access to alcohol was steadily being made more difficult, and the number of licensed taverns and stores reduced, the Ontario provincial government was not inclined to prohibit alcohol altogether. Ontario's pre-First World War Premier, Sir James Whitney, thought that quasi-religious issues such as temperance had no place in politics. Yet, the First World War would accomplish what battalions of temperance ministers had failed to do. Many of the existing licenses were revoked under the premise that grain was needed to feed the troops, not to distil alcohol. Going without liquor seemed to be a small sacrifice when so many of Canada's youth were giving their lives in Europe.

By 1916, two-thirds of Ontario's municipalities, almost all of them in rural areas, had total Prohibition. Later that year, the government of Premier William H. Hearst took the final step and made the entire province "dry." All bars would be closed, and liquor could only be sold for medicinal or sacramental purposes. "The war has changed everything," Hearst explained to the provincial legislature; the people demanded Prohibition. The *Ontario*

This *Toronto Globe* cartoon reacts with relief to the passage of Ontario's Temperance. The barroom had been trashed!

Temperance Act passed the legislature unanimously. While it remained legal to possess liquor, it could no longer be sold, and when the statute went into force on September 16, 1916, the province's saloons and hotels were forced to suspend service. [4] Yet, provincial laws could not infringe on federal powers over interprovincial and international commerce. Distilleries and breweries remained opened and produced their products much as before. The difference was that they could not sell their products in Ontario. The urgency to win the war led to further restrictions. In March 1918, Ottawa administered the final blow and by Order-in-Council prohibited (for the duration of the war) the shipping of liquor into any part of Canada (such as Ontario) in which alcohol was illegal. By law, Canada was now in the firm grip of Prohibition.

The Toronto *Globe*, long an advocate of temperance, exulted that "a dry Ontario will be a prosperous Ontario." In Windsor, the reaction was far from one of rejoicing.

2

AN INTEMPERATE CITY

During the evening of Saturday, September 16, 1916, the bars in Windsor were filled to capacity. "Wineclerks" bustled up and down the tables filling last orders before the taverns closed down for the duration of the war; or possibly longer:

> As the hands of the City's clocks slowly marked the passing of the 'wet' era the bartenders for the most part, forgot all about such minor things as taking in money and old customers were furnished with 'farewell drinks' without cost.[1]

As the dreaded closing hour of 7 p.m. approached, bottles were simply put out on the bar to be consumed. When one was finished, another took its place. Finally, at closing time, the crowd was herded out into the streets. However, unlike most of Ontario, Windsorites were only a five-minute ferry ride away from Detroit, Michigan and its lively bar scene.

In an ironic twist on what was to come, thirsty Canadians looked across the river to meet their needs.

Windsor and all the border communities had always had a warm relationship with alcohol. In the 1740s, French settlers had arrived as part of the *ancien regime* outpost at Fort Detroit. They planted a variety of orchards and from them they pressed ciders and distilled a potent "eau de vie." One of the area's few exports was "high wine," which was not wine at all but a distillate. In 1820, a Scottish doctor, John Howison, visited the south shore of the Detroit River and remarked on the abundance of fruit in every house he entered and that "cider abounds at the table." As a small boy in the 1880s, Walter Griffith recalled French women in their houses strung along the First Concession (later Tecumseh Road) washing, spinning, and carding wool into yarn, all the while "they would drink cider, sing songs, swap stories…"[2]

By the early twentieth century, the Canadian side of the Detroit River in the northwest corner of Essex County was composed of a number of distinct communities. Directly across from Detroit was the city of Windsor. Originally the site of a ferry crossing, Windsor had become a focal point for railways, and, more recently, metal and automotive industries. Windsor, with a 1920 population of almost 40,000, formed the nucleus of the border area, and was ringed by several autonomous municipalities. To its southwest lay the old frontier town of Sandwich, the former seat of district government. While Sandwich suffered by being off-centre from rail connections, it was beginning to develop a chemical industry, and there were prospects for its growth. To

Ouellette Avenue in downtown Windsor, looking south, circa 1920.

Windsor's east was Walkerville and the Hiram Walker distilleries. A Massachusetts man, Walker had started a grocery business in Detroit in 1838, and by 1850, owned his own general store. He began by manufacturing cider vinegar before moving to distilling spirits, a business he found provided maximum profits. But temperance was in full force in Michigan in the 1850s, and Walker moved across the Detroit River in 1856. There he ran a paternalistic but benevolent company town that established a reputation for the superiority of its product. Its premier brand, "Canadian Club," was hugely popular across North America, to the extent that its American competitors tried to use the pure food laws to prohibit it. They failed, and the Walker distillery remained highly profitable and one of the area's major employers.

The new dynamo for the region lay to the east of Walkerville, where a corner of Sandwich East Township became the site of one of Canada's largest auto assembly plants. Gordon McGregor, a local entrepreneur, had seen the potential of building an extension of the Ford auto assembly plant in Canada. Ford cars built in Windsor could be sold in Canada and across the British Empire without paying tariffs. For his part, Henry Ford, the rising giant in the American automotive industry, saw the prospect of accessing huge new markets in the British Empire from a factory that was only minutes away from his American operations. Under McGregor's direction, Ford of Canada became one of the most spectacularly successful branch plants. Its sales soared, and in 1920 the plant produced over 55,000 vehicles and sold them through a network of 685 dealerships. The factory site and its surrounding ring of residences was, fittingly enough, called "Ford City."[3] While these four communities (known as the "Border Cities") were contiguous to each other, and to the casual observer made up one metropolitan area, they guarded their autonomy and remained fiercely independent.

As so many of the Border Cities factories were American branch plants, it was inevitable that the region functioned as a unit. While technically divided by the international border, the Detroit-Windsor region often operated socially and economically as one district. Windsor residents manned Detroit factories and shops and vice versa. Families intermingled and intermarried across the border. Windsor residents took full advantage of Detroit's major league sports and off-Broadway shows, which were only a minute away. Cross-border traffic also came from the other direction, thanks again to the asymmetrical state of the laws between the parent countries. Religious zeal led to purity movements in Michigan and Ohio that banned horse-racing in the early twentieth century. Canadian authorities also prohibited gambling but provided an exception for periodic race meets. In July 1914, an estimated 15,000 punters (most of them Americans) came to Windsor to take in the races. Ferry boats were so packed with fans that customs officials could barely handle them. It was apparent that "In the minds of many locals the community was, culturally and economically, one with the city of Detroit and a part of the rapidly developing American industrial frontier."[4]

While it had much in common with Detroit, Windsor was different from the rest of the province in its ethnic and religious make-up. While most Ontario cities had a small French-Canadian presence, almost twenty percent of Windsor's population was French-speaking and Catholic. Sandwich was almost thirty-five percent French Canadian, and French was a common language on its streets. Eastern Europeans had also been attracted to Ford City's factories, and there were

Hiram Walker & Sons was established in 1858. Its booming liquor business created the town of Walkerville.

neighbourhoods which were entirely Polish or Russian. Ford City was perhaps the only large town in Ontario that had one Orthodox and one Catholic church and no Protestant church. Restricted to certain neighbourhoods such as the "Polish Colony" on Marion Street, Eastern European men lived in cramped boarding houses where they spoke their native languages and indulged in their usual drinks and customs.[5] With a population and religious mix that was so different from the rest of Ontario, the Border Cities' attitude towards the temperance issue was bound to vary from the provincial norm.

As the temperance movement gained ground in Ontario, and many rural areas chose to exercise the local option to prohibit alcohol, the border area headed in the opposite direction. The Reverend E.H. Dewar, the Anglican rector of Sandwich, heatedly complained in 1855 that the laws requiring taverns to close on Sunday were not being enforced. "Bar-rooms and taverns in both Windsor and Sandwich were all open. There was in both places, a lamentable profanation of the Sabbath." Yet even when constables attempted to enforce the laws, Windsor drinkers were only a short ferry ride away from Detroit's taverns. In 1873, it was reported that "at the (Detroit) Central Station on Monday of 34 cases of drunkenness one third of them were defended by Windsorites."

By the 1880s, when so much of the country was using the *Scott Act* to limit access to intoxicants, Windsor was making it easier to drink. In 1875, twenty-five taverns applied to the Council to conduct business in a town of 8,000 persons. One Council member thought nothing of authorizing this increase, for tavern-keeping "was like any other trade." In 1886, two new breweries were opened; one was founded by the Detroit brewer Louis Griesinger (and given the patriotic name the "British-American Brewery"), while the other was a subsidiary of Hiram Walker, the Walkerville Brewery. The Amherstburg newspaper the *Echo* noted the growing importance of whisky and beer production to the area's economy and concluded that "Windsor liquor men think that two new breweries in Windsor in a year means that the sentiment in favor of the Scott prohibition act in the county is not increasing."[6]

Not only were they making alcohol, border folk were consuming it with gusto. In 1887, it was reported that tavern owners were largely ignoring the regulations to the extent that closing-hour violations in Windsor were as bad as anywhere in Detroit. That same year, the *Echo* reported that the Sunday closing laws were not enforced in Windsor and that "An epidemic of drunkenness appears to have struck Windsor on Saturday…nearly all the cells were occupied." Even Parliament noticed that the Windsor area was different. Essex County's representative in the House of Commons, J.C. Patterson, came out against any extension of the *Scott Act*. Speaking as the representative of a riding in which so many workers and businessmen were occupied in distilling alcohol, he opposed such laws as they "are an interference with individual liberty; they are an interference with our civil rights" and that Canada should remain a nation "of free men." One wag across the aisle added: "free and drunk." This attitude was further confirmed in the provincial plebiscite on Prohibition in 1894. While there was an overwhelming 3-1 vote in its favour, and all Ontario cities gave majorities to Prohibition, Windsor was the lone exception.

Undeterred, local clergyman increasingly damned the local tolerance of liquor. Presbyterian pastor, the Reverend J.C. Tolmie, regularly castigated local officials for turning a blind eye to liquor infractions and for defying the provincial trend by increasing the number of licensed establishments. In 1903, Tolmie noted that the Border Cities had sixty licensed establishments, perhaps the highest concentration in the province. Two years later, there was a total of seventy-eight hotels and taverns in North Essex, and the local newspaper, the *Evening Record,* ruefully reported that "In Tecumseh, which is not even a village, only a few houses grouped around about a railway station, there were four licenses granted, two more than last year... Every road leading from these townships to Windsor is lined with taverns."[7]

After the founding of Ford of Canada in 1904, this trend was, if anything, accentuated. During working hours, Ford supervisors insisted on production, not chatter. But at the end of the shift, the saloon, or more likely the blind pig as the licensed saloons closed at 7 p.m., offered men a chance to relax. A Hamilton study in 1913 found that no women or professional men could be found in the city's bars. Women were confined to the household and businessmen socialized at private clubs. The saloons became the exclusive meeting place for wage earners where "A worker could find there an informal, relatively open community of sociability." When reformers attempted to further reduce the number of licenses in

Hamilton, a hotel-keeper explained that this would eliminate saloons which were "a social solvent and center."[8]

However, Windsor factory owners did not care about their worker's social needs. When in 1913, Arsas Drouillard, a member of the family that gave its name to the main road that ran through Ford City,

DRINK HELPS THE ENEMY!

"HE WHO IS FOR ALCOHOL IS AGAINST ENGLAND!"

In the great TUG-OF-WAR.
HELP BRITAIN - BY ABSTAINING *from* DRINK!

This 1915 editorial cartoon reflects the war's impact on the Prohibition cause. Abstaining from drink was no longer merely moral, it was patriotic.

applied for a liquor license, he ran into the determined opposition of the capitalists. Drouillard applied to open a tavern almost across from Ford's main gate, but found his application opposed by the company's founder, Gordon McGregor. McGregor, supported by a variety of other plant operators, argued that the "foreigners" on their assembly lines could not cope with strong liquor. Walter McGregor, Gordon's brother and the operator of a metal company, pointed out that the area just south of the Ford factory known as "Hungry Hollow" featured the "Dew Drop Inn," one of the worst dives west of Toronto. However, the workers clearly wanted Drouillard's tavern, and the license commission bowed to a petition that indicated strong public support for it. Unswayed, McGregor pulled political strings in Toronto and had the license revoked.

Nevertheless, beer had become a staple part of the life of many urban workers. While there had been a steady

27

movement away from hard liquors to lower content alcohol, most urban residents, especially in the Border Cities, expected to have access to drink. As a result, the *Evening Record*, which was devoted to the temperance cause, felt compelled to report on the dire situation. A 1912 editorial lamented that while the rest of Ontario had dutifully fallen in line with the government's plans to reduce licensed establishments, the border had stubbornly resisted. London, with double Windsor's population, had barely three more licensed taverns than Windsor. Indeed, the rate of licenses being issued was the highest in the province. Something needed to be done. The *Evening Record* suggested that Windsor's twenty-three licensed drinking spots be reduced to ten, for "the public is insisting on fewer and better hotels." Clearly, they were not, for the number of licenses being issued remained as high as ever.[9] It was a situation that engaged the attention of the local Methodist clergy. In September 1912, the Reverend S.L. Toll personally inspected a number of Windsor hotels and discovered that they were serving booze after hours. A number of charges resulted. But it was all temporary, and once the clergymen were gone, the bars and hotels returned to their normal practices.

All that changed when the First World War broke out in August 1914. Previously ignored moral laws began to be enforced, and Windsor was subjected to a crack-down on bringing Sunday newspapers across from Detroit. The *Lord's Day Act* prevented any publishing in Canada, so locals had grown accustomed to reading the massive Sunday edition of the *Detroit Free Press*. In November 1916, the provincial attorney general prevented the distribution of the Sunday *Free Press*. The restrictions were only starting. Prohibition was seen as a necessary war measure to insure that factory hands remained sober and dedicated to production. Food stuffs should be limited to supplies for the troops and war workers and not diverted into alcohol production. As a result, several venerable roadhouses that had served Essex County for decades were ordered closed. Wolfgang Feller's shanty "Wolf's" at Lesperance Road and Lake St. Clair, a popular haunt for American and Canadian sportsmen for many years, had to lock its doors in July 1915. It was followed by the closing of several other treasured drinking spots including Louis Hebert's "Abars" tavern as well as Stephen's Inn in the downtown. Little by little, access to alcohol was being throttled in the Border Cities. The final act was the imposition of the *Ontario Temperance Act* in 1916. In theory, the Border Cities had gone dry.[10]

The source of these unwelcome restrictions was the provincial capital, Toronto. Shortly after the end of the war, there was a crack-down on sports on Sunday. One returned soldier, Captain Brooks Baxter, spoke for many when he identified the cause of these unwelcome rules:

> We are being run by a clique which rules us from Toronto and I see no reason why we should be told what to do and what not to do by that little bunch down there.
>
> Over in France the boys played baseball on Sunday without any Lord's Day Alliance hanging around to tell them not to do it...

Wolf's Hotel, one of many area roadhouses, was forced to close in 1915, after government crackdowns on booze.

It was Toronto that would increasingly be the source of the laws that irked border residents.

Still, there was always Detroit. Windsor drinkers had found another reason (in addition to Broadway theatre and baseball) to spend their leisure time in America's fastest growing city. Almost two years after Prohibition had come into effect in Ontario, the *Evening Record* expressed its dismay at the spectacle that regularly presented itself at the ferry docks. The final boats returning from Detroit were loaded to the gunwales with pugnacious drunks, both male and female. To the customs officers, it was simply the "last boat fight" as per usual:

> The matter has reached that stage where it has become a public scandal. Visitors from eastern points are shocked at conditions they find, saying that the sights to be seen on the streets of Windsor during the late hours at night cannot be even approached in any other city in America...
>
> Conditions existing in Windsor have been made the subject of sermons preached by eastern clergymen

who had the opportunities of witnessing scenes which
the residents of the border seem to accept as a matter
of course.[11]

While border residents had an escape in Detroit, that
outlet was about to be shut tight as well. There had
always been a zealous temperance streak in Michigan.
In the 1850s, Michigan passed a prohibition law based
on the Maine statute, but by the late 1880s, legal
interpretations had so weakened the law that breweries
and distilleries were back in business. But in the early
twentieth century, the temperance movement found
a renewed vigour. Led by the "Anti-Saloon League of
America," temperance evolved into a social movement
that condemned the beer drinking culture that marked
the immigrant working class. The ASL concentrated
on specific legislation, and its sophisticated network
of speakers and publications made it a powerful lobby
against that corporate bogeyman, "the liquor interests."
Michigan temperance forces were energized, and
on November 7, 1916, voters approved state-wide
Prohibition to go into effect on April 30, 1918.

Detroit Police Commissioner James Couzens felt
that Prohibition would be a "great benefit" to the city,
purging it of crime and vice. Little would he suspect
that within a year Prohibition would have spawned
an entirely new industry for "despite all the rosy
predictions of 1919, the illegal sale of liquor not only
flourished in Detroit in the next decade, but eventually
came to dominate the commercial life of the city."[12]
Nevertheless, J.D. Flavelle, the chairman of the Ontario
Board of License Commissioners, saw it as an auspicious

event: "Prohibition in effect in Michigan will mean more effective enforcement of the Ontario act in that quarter." Not for the last time, Flavelle would be hugely mistaken in his evaluation of the situation.

3

FIGHTERS

Ironically, both of the families involved in the impending tragedy came from Woodstock. Joseph Spracklin, an English-born harness maker, had first set up in Woodstock, relocated briefly to Chatham, and finally settled in Windsor around 1896. The border area had become a hotbed of horseracing and Spracklin got a job as a saddler at one of the tracks. To supplement his income, he raised hunting dogs and game chickens. While their resources were modest, the Spracklins were a large family with two daughters and four sons: Gerald, Arthur, William, and John Oswald Leslie (familiarly known as "Leslie"). Born in Woodstock in December 1886, Leslie went to primary school in Chatham before the family put down roots in Windsor.

On June 2, 1886, Beverley Clarence "Babe" Trumble was also born in Woodstock. About five years later, his father Hamilton "Ham" Trumble moved his family to Windsor. Unlike Joseph Spracklin, who worked in a low-paying occupation, Ham Trumble was a baker and confectioner whose pastries and treats provided his family with a comfortable living. The mothers, Helen Trumble and Charity Spracklin, had known each other well in Woodstock and their friendship continued in Windsor.

In 1920, in the wake of the Chappell House shooting, a Detroit newspaper gathered together several men who had known both families and could recall the rough and tumble of life on the school yards of Windsor. Fighting was a rite of passage for boys, and neither Leslie Spracklin nor Babe Trumble were adverse to it. Leslie at the Cameron School and Babe at Central were gang leaders and "both boys were good fighters and liked clean sport" one man recalled. "There was only one difference between them, Leslie never knew when he was licked, and Babe was a 'one punch' fighter. Babe was always feared by his opponents. They knew he carried a good punch and he was respected for it." Star Mason, a well-known local sports figure, thought that there was always a bitter feeling between boys from the two schools, and that inevitably their leaders would be drawn into brawls. Mason felt that "Trumble wasn't what you would call a fighting kid. He could fight when pressed and could fight hard," but on the other hand, "Leslie seemed to love to fight." When not roaming the streets, boys would congregate at the Trumble bakery where Mrs. Trumble freely supplied George Washington buns to poorer boys such as the Spracklins.[1]

Despite their low economic status, fighting was one way in which the Spracklins first came to public notice. Leslie's older brother Willie was a tough young featherweight boxer who began to fight professionally in 1903. In 1906, he had a sensational match against Frank Carsey of Cleveland that lasted twenty-five rounds and ended in a draw. However, prize fighting was illegal in Ontario, and a vigilant Essex County Crown Attorney, J.H. Rodd, broke up a Spracklin fight scheduled in the county for March 1906. Rodd, who would later figure prominently in support of Willie's brother Leslie, had been the area's Crown Attorney since 1904. A vigorous defender of the moral laws, Rodd would be quick to lay charges to prevent baseball on Sundays, prize fights, or blind pigs near factories.

It is ironic that the Spracklin name, which came to represent an aggressive defence of all things righteous, was previously associated with so many shady activities. Joseph's occupation as a saddler was intimately tied into horseracing, a pastime that was condemned by many preachers. In 1916, at the Central Methodist Church, the Reverend W.E. Prescott gave a resounding sermon condemning racetracks, for "No institution fosters gambling like horse racing." Joseph's son Willie ("Sprack" as he was known to the reporters) was becoming a prominent name in the sports pages across the Midwest, but was following a career that was illegal in his home country and most American states. However questionable the Spracklin background, there was no denying that Willie had a huge following among the young bloods of the city. Yet his career came to a halt in late 1906 when Mike Ward, one of his closest friends, died after a bout in Grand Rapids, Michigan. Depressed, Willie considered retiring from the ring. Almost a year later, he was duck hunting on Fighting Island when he was accidentally shot and killed by his friend Star Mason. Questions were raised that alcohol may have played a part in the accident.[2]

Willie's sudden, violent death shocked his brother. Since leaving school in 1902, Leslie had worked in a variety of jobs, but increasingly found work as a machinist in Windsor or Detroit. Most boys did not stay in school past the age of fourteen, so it was not unusual that he was out in the world at that age. Like many other young men, he eventually found work at the Ford auto assembly plant. Even at that stage of his life, he stood out. One of his co-workers recalled that he was "pleasant to everyone, but not much of a socializer. When the other workers went out to the bars on payday, he never joined them... He didn't drink or swear... he would tell off any man who swore in front of a lady."[3] Willie's death awakened a spiritual need, and Leslie felt a calling to become a preacher of the Methodist Church. But his limited education was a handicap. In 1909, perhaps to test whether or not his vocation was real, Spracklin was sent by the Church to the Port Lambton circuit. Church authorities were satisfied that he was genuine and he was enrolled at the Windsor Collegiate Institute to complete his matriculation.

At the same time as Spracklin received his call, the Methodist Church in Canada was undergoing a profound struggle with modernism. In 1909, the Reverend George Jackson of Toronto suggested that a literal reading of the book of Genesis was no longer tenable. He was rebuked by Dr. Albert Carman who upheld the literalist view and suggested that what Methodism needed was fire-breathing preachers, not effete scholars. Spracklin may or may not have paid much notice to the Carman-Jackson controversy, for as an aspiring Methodist preacher, he was aligning himself with the heart of the Prohibition movement. It had not always been so. For in the early 1800s, the Methodist Church had tolerated moderate drinking, but as the century advanced, Methodism became a powerful force for the transformation of Canada into a moral society. The church's support of prohibition played an emotional and aggressive role in evangelizing the nation and making it into a finer place by abolishing the poison of alcohol. For Methodists, abstinence was not a matter of personal choice. Alcohol, any alcohol, even in the form of wine or beer, was a toxin that shattered the national fabric and must be abolished. As later events would show, young Spracklin was eager to play his part in this crusade, the "linchpin of all reform."[4]

Since the late 1800s, Protestant ministers had spearheaded the temperance cause along the border. While it may have seemed to be a losing cause in such an irredeemably intemperate area, Windsor preachers could be counted on to give thunderous sermons whenever there was a temperance plebiscite to be voted on. In 1902, both Reverend J.C. Tolmie in the Presbyterian church of St. Andrew, and the Reverend Bovington in the Baptist church, urged their followers to vote for the *Liquor Act* to

Methodism was a powerful force in Canadian life. Here, the 1878 Methodist Church Conference of Canada is depicted.

close down the saloons. Bovington emphasized that this was no longer an issue of personal restraint, for it was time that "the state should guard the homes from evil." This might have resonated with his congregation, but electors in North Essex voted almost four to one against liquor controls. Nevertheless, militant evangelism occasionally asserted itself in Windsor's churches. In 1916, Adjutant W. Squarebriggs gave a blood and thunder denunciation of the evils of modern society in the Salvation Army Citadel. He denounced Windsor's vices, which included "the dance hall, the race tracks, lack of home training and 'the oyster supper' kind of religion." Furthermore the area had to wrestle with a "damnable curse- These gambling race tracks outside our city are a blot on Windsor's name." Squarebriggs concluded that modern life was plain rotten and what "Windsor wants more of the terror-striking preaching and less of the loose theological arguments of the devil known as higher criticism."[5]

Not all preachers who were concerned with their flock's morality were Protestants. Father Lucien Beaudoin, the long-time pastor of Our Lady of the Rosary (formerly *Notre Dame du Lac*) Church in Ford City, was concerned about his people's exposure to the urban drinking culture. In 1909, he criticized the free issuance of licenses which had resulted in local hotels becoming drinking holes for "thirsty young men, farmers." During the controversy over the Arsas Drouillard license petition in 1913, Beaudoin had explained to the commissioners that "This saloon will be the ruin of the working people of this neighborhood. They are all poor people coming from the country... The only thing to raise the standard of these people is for them to practice temperance." French-Canadians making the short move of only a few miles from the farms of northern Essex County to the factories of the Border Cities faced an enormous culture shock of having to work in an English-speaking environment and according to a clock and not to the rhythms of the countryside. Yet, Beaudoin also appreciated that they came from a culture where alcohol was a way of life. As opposed to his Methodist or Presbyterian colleagues, he felt that "it is my duty as a priest to promote temperance- not prohibition, but temperance in my parish."[6]

However, to mainstream Protestant leaders, nothing less than the complete abolition of the bar, and a halt to the sale of liquor, wine, and beer was the ultimate objective. And of all the denominations advocating the cause, none could match the fervour of the Methodists. In 1911, Windsor's Central Methodist Church was packed to hear the Irish evangelist, Reverend C. Jeff McCombe, give a fire and brimstone speech against "Windsor's greatest devil- the open licensed saloon." The following year, the Reverend S.L. Toll of the London Street Methodist Church struck a blow even closer to home when he gave an extended sermon that accused Windsor police of deliberately overlooking the evils of the liquor trade. While he stopped just short of accusing them of accepting bribes, he stated that the police knew of illegal liquor houses and places serving after hours, and that they were doing nothing about it:

> It is commonly said that anyone can get liquor at almost any bar in the city at any time. There is no

question that there is something wrong with the civic administration of Windsor...[7]

As an aspiring Methodist preacher, Spracklin was joining a strong tradition of vigorous advocacy of temperance. As Toll was making his denunciation, Spracklin had just started his theological training at Victoria College, Toronto. His studies were interrupted by a return to Windsor for a year to take charge of the Howard Avenue mission. This interlude seems unusual for a clergyman in training who had yet to complete his studies. In any case, he returned to Victoria College, graduated in theology, and was ordained in the town of Kingsville in 1916, the same year the temperance cause prevailed. But it needed muscular and determined enforcers to ensure its enduring victory.

The Trumbles had also made a name for themselves, but in ways far different from the Spracklins. As the well-liked owner of a bake shop, Ham Trumble was a popular figure in Windsor's Third Ward, and after 1903, he would regularly be elected to City Council. He was constantly in conflict with fellow council members, and during one confrontation in 1904, he was ordered by

TRUMBLE EGGED EANSOR INTO HOT DISCUSSION

Proceedings at Council Meeting Enlivened by Tilt Over that Extra Light on Sandwich Street—No Language Used Stronger Than 'Four—Flusher'.

This 1909 article hints at Hamilton Trumble's notoriety during his time as an alderman on City Council.

the Mayor to restrain himself. Trumble shouted back, "I won't leave the room nor I won't keep order." Keeping in order seemed beyond Ham Trumble's capacity. In 1906, he was re-elected but denied any significant committee seats by his colleagues. In May, the reason for his exclusion became clear when Trumble almost started a brawl on the Council floor. But perhaps the pinnacle of his infamy came in 1910 when he sought to test the fire department's readiness by pulling an alarm signal. Convicted and fined for initiating a false alarm, he was rebuked by a magistrate for his reckless endangerment of the public. Still, he was beyond learning. Moments after his conviction, Trumble swore a complaint against the Fire Chief.

Young Babe Trumble finished school at about the same time as Leslie and began to work as a driver. Later, he drifted into a variety of jobs including house painting, and for a period he seems to have left Windsor and tried his luck elsewhere. An incident occurred just before the outbreak of the First World War which revealed that he had inherited much of father's fiery disposition. On the high ground just behind the ferry dock to Detroit, Babe witnessed an accident between a motorcycle and a taxi. As a policeman attempted to arrest one of the parties, Trumble shouted out a warning. When the officer called out that he should move on and mind his own business, Trumble hurled defiance and suggested that the officer make him. He did. Constable Monroe administered a thorough thrashing and arrested him to boot.[8]

Both Leslie Spracklin and Babe Trumble resisted any patriotic impulses to serve in the First World War. Perhaps they were too involved with their own lives.

After his ordination, Leslie became the pastor to a small congregation in the southwestern Ontario town of Romney. His new position enabled him to support a family, and on June 17, 1917, he married Myrle Welsh. In September 1918, only a few weeks before the war ended, Spracklin was transferred to the Methodist Church in Sandwich. While technically a small town, Sandwich was part of the Windsor metropolitan area and only a short cab ride away from the ferry to Detroit. He found himself and his small family living only a few miles from where he had grown up, in an area that was now urbanized, secular, and in many ways hostile to the morality preached by his Church. Ironically, Babe Trumble, recently married and with a son, Robert, born in 1919, also settled in Sandwich. But in Trumble's case, the easy-going morality of the urban area was something he hoped to profit from.

In the summer of 1919, Trumble acquired the Chappell House at the western limit of Sandwich. The Chappell property had been the site of the thoroughbred

Sandwich Methodist Church, pictured here in 1915, was Spracklin's parish in the early 1920s.

farm of Henry and his brother Harley. Originally from Rochester, New York, the brothers found the flat lands of Sandwich West Township ideal for raising race horses, and were so successful that some of their horses competed in the Queen's Plate in Toronto. As an adjunct to their breeding program, the Chappells operated a hotel along what was then Bedford Street. As a "roadhouse," it catered to travelers, particularly those on the road from Windsor heading south to Amherstburg. The hotel was a popular venue, and provided livery stables in the back for horses as well as accommodation and beverages for thirsty travelers. When it appeared that U.S. Steel would build a huge complex adjacent to them in Ojibway, the Chappell brothers moved closer to Sandwich town centre. In 1903, a new brick hotel with a wide, inviting verandah was erected. After Henry died in 1906, the Chappell House was run by his widow Frances. During the war years, the house gained a lawless reputation and was cited several times for violations of the *Ontario Temperance Act.*[9]

A Detroit *News* reporter recalled that "The Chappell House's very name conjures up well nigh a century of Border history." In addition to its fish, chicken, and frog legs dinners, it was renowned "for the free and easy atmosphere, with which the place was always surrounded... The coming of prohibition enhanced rather than diminished the abandon that has ever been one of the resort's chief expectations."[10] In 1919, perhaps due to her advancing age, Frances sold out to Hamilton and Beverley Trumble. While his father helped finance the acquisition, it was Babe who would operate the roadhouse. Advertising that it was "Under

New Management," the Chappell House offered frogs legs and chicken dinners to prospective customers. As the hotel had no license, it could not even advertise that it sold legal, low-alcohol "near beer." While the Chappell House presented a show of uprightness, as events would prove, Babe Trumble had no intention of restoring it to respectability.

With the armistice of November 11, 1918, many hoped for an easing of the government's role in controlling their lives. Conscription and temperance had been new and unwelcome intrusions. In this first Christmas of peace after more than four years of war, many people along the Detroit River border hoped that they could truly celebrate. But with the iron hoops of temperance firmly in place, how would this be possible?

A 1919 advertisement for Babe Trumble's Chappell House.

4

ENFORCING
TEMPERANCE

Just before Christmas 1918, the office of Dr. G.N. Gardner at 246½ Gladstone Avenue in Windsor was being besieged by patients. Lines of men snaked down the street as they waited patiently to gain admittance. The Spanish Influenza had ripped through the Border Cities from October 1918 to mid-December and taken about 250 lives. However, the men laying siege to Dr. Gardner's medical practice looked healthy enough, and all of them were after one thing. The *OTA* had provided an exemption for alcohol prescribed by a medical professional for therapeutic reasons, and in July 1918, the Province authorized a Windsor liquor store to fill these prescriptions. It was an instant success. Hundreds of medical forms (the most popular one explaining that the sufferer had endured a snake bite) authorized the issuance of a flood of alcohol. Canada's pre-eminent satirist, and a confirmed drinker, Stephen Leacock, wrote that in order to get a drink in Ontario it was now necessary "to go to a drugstore, and lean up against the counter and make a gurgling sound like apoplexy. One often sees these apoplexy cases lined up four deep."

They were certainly lined up along Gladstone Avenue in the hope that Dr. Gardner would fill their pre-Christmas orders. As the *Border Cities Star* recounted in an editorial entitled "The Prohibition Farce," holiday shoppers stood in front of the liquor vendor's store with prescriptions in hand. "Old and young, young women as well as young men stood in line. It resembled a first night theatre line-up." Eventually, the Essex County Medical Society cracked down on its members and reminded them that they were medical professionals and not instruments of the liquor trade. But some practitioners remained eminently pliable and the drinking class gravitated to their doors. On January 2, 1919, Gardner was charged with issuing "unnecessary" prescriptions and the following week stood trial before Magistrate Alfred Miers. One of Dr. Gardner's "patients" who testified for the prosecution was a young Air Force officer, Lt. Arthur Spracklin. Having finished his military service, Arthur (Leslie's younger brother) was also destined for the Methodist pulpit. But before entering the clergy, he wanted to perform a service for the temperance cause. Upon entering the Doctor's surgery, Spracklin lied to Gardner and told him that he had a pain in his chest. Gardner then asked if a quart of whisky would be enough. Spracklin noted that at no time had he asked for any liquor, nor did Gardner pause to actually examine him. In fact, the door of his consulting room was left open as men were coming and going one after the other. The magistrate concluded that the sole purpose of Gardner's medical practice was to issue prescriptions for liquor and fined him $200 and costs.[1] A few weeks later, another Windsor doctor, I.N. Cherniak, was convicted of violating the *OTA* and his medical license was revoked. The open tap on getting medical prescriptions for alcohol was steadily being squeezed shut, and drinkers were forced to search elsewhere.

This could be a challenge for "In 1919 the prohibitionists were on top…through years of experience, the prohibitionists had become masters of the art of propaganda. Their leading argument and their justification for political action was the principle 'the tighter the law the fewer get tight.'"[2] Temperance had a new ally, for recently enfranchised women were heavily in support of continuing Prohibition. The temperance cause would also continue to have the unswerving support of the Methodist Church and its powerful newspaper the *Christian Guardian.* The men and women who fought for temperance were sincere in their beliefs and hopeful that they were creating a better society; and now they held the political upper hand.

However, they would face one intractable problem. The rise of cities such as Windsor, Hamilton, and Toronto meant that there was a growing majority that favoured a more relaxed attitude towards drinking. As the seat of provincial government, Toronto was a unique case. A city of church spires, where Anglican, Presbyterian, and Methodist churches shot towers into the sky, Toronto had acquired the sobriquet "Toronto the Good." The nickname appears to have originated during the tenure of anti-vice mayor, William Howland, in the 1880s. However, even from the beginning, the nickname was a misnomer, steeped in satire. As journalist C.S. Clark described it in his 1898 exposé, Toronto was also the home for scores of brothels and unlicensed drinking spots. Adolescents smoked and drank and entire neighbourhoods were given over to prostitutes. By the 1920s, Toronto was a burgeoning metropolis, fueled by factory workers who expected refreshment after a grueling day and could not see why they should be denied. Still, conservative politicians, religious reformers, and much of the Toronto press were set on keeping up appearances, even as the city around them became increasingly cosmopolitan.

If Ontario's cities, including the provincial capital, were increasingly wet, the province's true social divide was between its rural and urban communities. In the early years of the twentieth century, Ontario remained very much an agrarian province. The farming community remained "the sheet anchor of the country."

Toronto, circa 1920.

This agrarian society was overwhelmingly British and Protestant and strongly backed moral reform by government action. In contrast to rural Ontario, Windsor had a diverse ethnic make-up which resulted in a different set of values where temperance was concerned. The 1921 census showed that Windsor and its industrial border neighbour of Ford City were barely sixty percent British, and contained a significant Catholic population. The Border Cities had a leaven of Eastern Europeans and French Canadians who had no use for Prohibition, and who regularly consumed low-percentage alcohol as a regular and pleasurable part of daily life. This diversity presented a clear danger. In 1914, one Methodist leader warned that unless Prohibition was soon imposed that the incoming numbers of foreigners "with their love for strong drink, with their life-long habits of using it" would overwhelm Ontario's native Protestants and make future temperance laws impossible. For better or worse, this state of affairs had already happened in Windsor.[3]

Added to this social discord was the feeling among many of the area's returned soldiers that they had been betrayed. These men, who has seen and experienced so much overseas, had returned to a community in which so many of their favourite recreations were now banned. Not only did they want them back, they wanted an end to the enforced morality of the war years. The Detroit River border would increasingly become the focal point for this conflict between the moral uplift of the temperance movement and an emerging leisure- and consumer-oriented society.

On the morning of Monday, August 17, 1919, a crowd gathered around an old-fashioned brewery wagon parked on Ouellette Avenue as the almost-forgotten, pungent smells of whisky permeated the air. Onlookers marveled as police unloaded case after case of liquor from the wagon and carried the heavy loads up to the safe in the office of License Inspector M.N. Mousseau. In all, eighty-six cases containing twelve bottles each, or 1,032 quarts of fine whisky worth $10,000 were deposited into custody. The precious cargo had been on a freight car from Quebec and marked as "apples" bound for Dominion Canners in Tecumseh. Mousseau had been tipped off about the shipment, and on Monday his men swooped in to make the seizure. All through the summer, the *Border Cities Star* had been running reports about the "cornstarch trail" of liquor shipments from Quebec. But the destination of the "apple" shipment was not the Border Cities, but the lucrative market of Detroit. While that Michigan city was theoretically under the grip of state-mandated Prohibition, it was as wet as ever and drinking was as widespread as if no laws had ever been passed.

Much like the Border Cities, Detroit's ethnic composition was at odds with its compatriots. Detroit had a substantial German presence to the extent that German was frequently heard on its streets and German-language newspapers were widely circulated. In 1890, forty-three percent of Detroit's population was German-born. While this proportion declined, to under thirty percent by 1910, the city was still heavily influenced by a population that inherited a European tolerance for and enjoyment of beer.[4] To the vast majority of Detroiters, indulging in beer was one of life's blessings, not a sin, and it should not be illegal. Yet, state Prohibition had already been in effect since 1918 and, with the passage of a constitutional amendment, the noose was about to be drawn even tighter.

Some thought that Mousseau's daring raid had stopped up the source of the booze "which has almost continuously flowed in some mysterious way eastward from Quebec into the deserts of Windsor and Detroit." Any illusions that the raid had actually plugged up the source of alcohol was quickly dispensed with during the prosecution of the accused whisky smuggler. Louis Kirsch, the proprietor of the Lakeside Hotel, appeared in Court two days after the seizure, denied that Dominion Canners was in any way involved, and accepted full responsibility for the offence. Before leaving the courtroom, he cheerfully paid the $1,000 fine. It was obvious to casual observers that Kirsch was playing his part on behalf of others and that he was only a small functionary in a much larger organization. The loss of this one shipment and the payment of a fine was only a paltry business expense in what was a "big ring that operates across the other side of the river."[5]

What the people of the Border Cities actually thought about the emerging illegal trade in liquor became apparent in October 1919. In addition to the provincial election scheduled for that month, Premier Hearst added a referendum that posed four questions. First, voters were asked if they wanted to repeal the *OTA*. Then they had to express an opinion as to whether they were in favour of the sale of low-alcohol 2.5% "near" beer, the beverage that quickly bloated the imbiber without providing any satisfying result. The final questions asked if the voters accepted the sale of near beer in hotels and finally whether they supported the sale of liquor and real beer through government agencies. W.F. Herman, the new proprietor of the municipality's leading newspaper, the *Border Cities Star*, was firmly in the temperance camp and argued that this great reform should be continued. The *Christian Guardian* warned that the referendum would be "the most momentous fight in the history of the Province of Ontario, and we trust…Ontario will go dry forever."

Yet, it was at a turbulent mass meeting held at the Windsor Collegiate Institute that all of Windsor's deeply held feelings on Ontario's temperance laws boiled to the surface. Almost 3,000 people jammed into the school to hear a lawyer, A.F. Healy of the Citizens Liberty League, argue the case against Prohibition. Healy maintained that at the very least, citizens should have the chance to indulge in light wine and beer. It was a question of "the liberty of a man to take a glass of beer if he wished." Hughson Johnstone, a prominent local organizer, championed the dry cause. He castigated his opponents for suggesting that they only wanted to reinstate beer sales. "We are told that beer is harmless, that it hasn't any kick… if it hasn't any kick, what do they want it back for." His supporters burst out in laughter. But unexpectedly, it was the audience members who seized control of the debate. None of the speakers could make much headway as they were constantly compelled to respond to hecklers from either faction. Perhaps most vocal in attacking the dry speakers was a large contingent of returned soldiers. At one point they tried to seize the floor and a veteran called out: "We won the war on rum rations, not on two-and-a-half percent beer." This was greeted by laughter and cheers. Another soldier added: "Now they tell us we ought to have wine and beer back. You'd need a little yourself if you were in ten feet of mud." The crowd cheered again. Johnstone tried to counter with statistics on crime and scriptural allusions, but he had clearly lost the evening to the veterans.[6]

On election night, Monday, October 20, 1919, an enormous crowd gathered in front of the *Border Cities Star* building on Ferry Street where the results were publicly displayed on a large screen hung on an adjacent building. The "wets" and the "drys" in the crowd were divided into hostile camps and cheered when any results were posted which advanced their side. The wets did most of the cheering as all of the questions to get rid of the *OTA* and to permit the resumption of sales of liquor and malt beer were approved by local voters by wide margins. The eastern part of the Border Cities, which was heavily French Canadian, voted almost unanimously against the *OTA*. But, true to form, the Border Cities were out of step with the rest of Ontario. The rural vote was overwhelmingly in favour of keeping

A LONG SUFFERING GOAT

This editorial cartoon from *Toronto World* illustrates the Conversative government's ousting by the United Farmers of Ontario in 1919.

Prohibition and disallowing any return of liquor sales. The dry side attracted enough urban support to get an overall majority. The Toronto *Globe* claimed it as another triumph for virtue, and attributed the few setbacks to the ethnics such as Germans in Kitchener or the French Canadians in Windsor.

While upholding Prohibition might have been predictable, to the surprise of many the Conservative government was defeated by the United Farmers of Ontario. That party, more of an agrarian protest movement than a political faction, sought to end corruption, supported extending rural electrification, and was unequivocally against liquor. Farm leaders felt they were on a mission to uplift the moral order of Ontario by imposing a firm enforcement of the temperance laws. If given the chance, the United Farmers would have outlawed the manufacture, sale, and consumption of alcohol altogether. The rural faction was now completely in the ascendancy, and it would have a profound effect on the situation on the Detroit River border.

In order to understand the confrontation at the Chappell House on November 6, 1920, it is important to appreciate the differences in the legal systems that operated on either side of the Detroit River. While a similar religious fervor stimulated temperance agitation on both sides of the border, it resulted in two distinct forms of legal controls. While national plebiscites in the 1890s and 1900s had supported Prohibition, Canada was starkly divided, and most urban areas and Quebec firmly opposed the measure. There would be no national Prohibition in Canada. Instead, a series of decisions from the Supreme Court defined the federal government's role in regulating the manufacturing as well as the interprovincial and international sale of alcohol. The provinces were limited to regulating matters of local concern such as licensing and internal sales. Therefore, under Canadian Prohibition during the First World War, Ontario still had forty-four breweries and nine distilleries, and Canada as a whole exported two million proof gallons of alcohol in 1921. In Canada, Prohibition was largely a commercial matter in which the manufacture of alcohol remained legal (except for a short period during the war) under federal law, while the retail sale was forbidden by most provinces. As each province set out its standards, there was a patchwork across the country with provinces such as British Columbia and Quebec permitting the sale of mail-order liquor to dry provinces such as Ontario.

When the federal war-time restriction on imports expired on January 1, 1920, access to alcohol was made easier, and the mail order business enabled drinkers to obtain what they wanted simply by posting a letter to a liquor outlet outside of Ontario.[7] In Windsor that meant that consumers could send an order to Detroit for whisky which would be duly delivered by Hiram Walker's distillery to the person requesting. As this was an international transaction it violated no provincial law. It was absurd, but legal, and it meant that Windsor residents now had access to unlimited amounts of alcohol.

Across the river in the United States, legal developments followed a very different course. The powerful Anti-Saloon League convinced Congress to pass the Eighteenth Amendment to the U.S. Constitution which totally prohibited the manufacture, sale, or transportation of intoxicating liquors. The Eighteenth Amendment became law in January 1918 and the subsequent *Volstead Act* set out a national prohibition code that effectively prohibited not only liquor, but wine and beer as well. Unlike Canada, the United States had become totally and pervasively dry. But enforcement was another matter, and Congress made little effort to supply the funds to implement Prohibition. The Treasury Department created a minuscule force of 1,550 agents to patrol the border and the Coast Guard was not strengthened at all.[8]

This lack of resources meant that in cities such as Detroit the law was one thing and reality another. James Couzens, who as Police Commissioner had been so optimistic over the prospects of Prohibition in 1918, became Detroit's Mayor the following year and had come to terms with the enforcement problem. Providing essential services such as education and sanitation to an exploding population was difficult enough. Dedicating scarce police resources to stop the sale of beer was a low priority indeed. Moreover, trying to keep an industrial work force from indulging in their usual refreshments was all but impossible. "Couzens concluded that a large city with a wet temperament could not be dried up…some kind of compromise with the prohibition law was necessary." That compromise meant that some discrete sales of alcoholic beverages would be tolerated by Detroit authorities. Blind pigs, so long as they were orderly and not near schools, operated largely without interference. Detroit had made a separate peace with Prohibition, and as historian Larry Engelmann concluded, "The drys still had their law, the wets still had their booze and the general public still had order."[9]

It was now a question of supply.

January 1, 1920, was not only the start of a new year, it also seemed to be the start of a vast new industry. With Prohibition officially the law of the United States and Canadian alcohol laws loosened to the effect that citizens could once again obtain liquor, there was a confluence of events that would create an entirely new phenomenon. "Rumrunner," a previously unheard of term, entered the lexicon. The asymmetry between American and Canadian laws had created a highly advantageous situation for the daring entrepreneur. Within days of national Prohibition coming into effect, Detroit customs authorities were stopping scores of Detroiters returning from Windsor with bulging pockets, claiming that they had a right to bring over "just one bottle." Three weeks into Prohibition, the *Detroit Free Press* reported that a major liquor shipment labeled as "whitefish" came across by rail.[10] Ambitious Canadians saw a thirsty, well-heeled population across the thin divide of the Detroit River and they rose to the challenge of meeting their demands.

In the beginning, there was a primitive, almost innocent feeling to the rumrunning trade. The *Star* described "the sweet, demure little maid with a bottle tied under her skirts, the cripple with liquor hidden in the rubber tires of his wheel chair" or a liquor bottle hidden among a baby's swaddling clothes. It was said that at least one hundred quarts of whisky were smuggled across to Detroit with every ferry passage. Surprisingly, the incidence of drunkenness was on the decline on the streets of the Border Cities. When a quart of whisky could be bought by mail order for one dollar

Liquor smugglers were always looking for creative ways to sneak booze across the border. Here, a woman shows off her retrofitted petticoat, capable of storing many bottles.

in Windsor and then sold in Detroit for eight to ten dollars, the inclination to actually consume it on the Canadian side declined substantially. Within two weeks of the start of the mail order business, the Border Cities were getting huge shipments of liquor. Over 1,500 quarts arrived each day, or one bottle for each man, woman, and child in the municipality for a month. So much was flowing in that it was apparent that "Detroiters are helping to consume the liquor."

By February, liquor inspector M.N. Mousseau was trying to clamp down, but whisky running had become rampant. Operating without weapons and using only his fists, Mousseau was conducting a number of raids and seizing hundreds of gallons of liquor. During one raid on a Dougall Avenue home, Mousseau was struck down and arrested only two of the four bootleggers. Significantly, the arrested men were all Detroiters. The only thing holding back so many Detroit residents from crossing over to Canada and taking advantage of the easy availability of booze was a recent smallpox outbreak. Until the middle of March 1920, anyone crossing the border had to show proof of vaccination. Once this stricture was lifted, it seemed that there was a tidal swell of Detroiters crossing the border to quench their thirst. On Monday mornings, most of the persons before the Court charged with *OTA* offences hailed from Detroit.

For those Michigan residents who wanted to drink but did not feel like leaving home, there was always the local speakeasy supplied by rumrunners from the Canadian side. It was reported that all along the river, operators were waiting for nightfall and then signaling drivers to come across the frozen river with their lights out. Evading the police on either side was only one of the dangers, for in February 1920, it was reported that one car laden with liquor had gone through the ice and disappeared with its cargo and occupants. Magistrate Miers admonished one bootlegger that his actions were dragging the area down into disrepute: "From all the cases of breaches of the Ontario temperance act that have been up before this court recently, the rest of Canada is beginning to look upon this community as a lawless centre."[11] The Magistrate did have mercy on one bootlegger who pleaded that he had a large family. In the circumstances, Miers reduced the fine from $500 to $400. Moments later, the convict's wife "pulled out a roll of greenbacks which fairly made the court gasp" and paid the fine in full.

By April, it was apparent that the situation was getting out of hand. A committee of the Citizens' Liberty League, an anti-temperance organization, went to Toronto to beg that this lawlessness be stopped. The head of the Liquor Licensing Department, J.D. Flavelle pointed out that Windsor Police were being less than co-operative with Liquor Inspector Mousseau. Flavelle noted that in Toronto, most of the arrests were made by the municipal police. In Windsor, it appeared that Mousseau was pretty much on his own. The Committee replied that one inspector was hardly adequate to control this long, volatile border. One senior police inspector stated that in only a few weeks, the dynamics of the situation along the border had changed. Bootlegging was ceasing to be the occasional romp across the river. Rather, it was becoming organized by a new class of "thugs" who were systematically amassing large stockpiles of liquor to be shipped across to the United States. What was needed was a special "O.T.A. force" under the direction of License Inspector Mousseau. Officers from this force would be stationed at the ferry crossing to somehow identify and exclude "this class of (Detroit) men…who will drink anything from bay rum to Florida water, as long as it contained alcohol."[12]

By the summer of 1920, the *Detroit News* was reporting that bootlegging was fueling a vibrant nightlife in the clubs that lined Lake St. Clair in Macomb County, Michigan. At Margolies Inn or the Denmarsh

Bootlegging was a growing, but dangerous, enterprise. Here, a partially-submerged car laden with beer was abandoned on Lake St. Clair, on route to Michigan.

Hotel, dancing, drinking, and gambling went on into the morning hours. "I wonder if it (Macomb County) will ever go dry again?" one young lady mused, and added, "Without doubt this is one of the wettest spots in the United States." Several weeks later, the *News* gave an account of a Canadian vessel from Tecumseh, Ontario, caught unloading liquor at Grosse Pointe Shores, Michigan.[13] The reporters attributed this unique victory to the brazenness of the bootleggers in making a shipment during a full moon. Despite this one loss, the clubs could rely on a regular supply of Canadian whisky, as well as the more questionable product from local stills. The industry had even changed the face of Michigan's communities. The downriver municipality of Ecorse (geographically closer to the Canadian town of LaSalle than to Detroit) had prior to Prohibition been a non-descript town. As a result of the rumrunning boom it became "a kind of glamorous gold camp, and gained a reputation as the most corrupt community in the state."[14]

In the meantime, Magistrate Miers was hearing *OTA* cases from morning till evening and imposing fines at a rate never seen before. In one week, the provincial government was raking in almost as much fine revenue in the Border Cities than it made in the area during an entire year. A typical case was that of Isadore Katzman. Near the end of April, he was charged with selling seventy-five cases of whisky. Katzman's defence was that this was his liquor reserve in case the provision permitting mail-order alcohol was revoked. Carelessly, he had left his home unlocked, and his stash had been stolen from his basement. Crown Attorney

John Rodd pointed out that Katzman had been absent on the night of the alleged theft and, suspiciously, his premises were left open. Magistrate Miers convicted Katzman on the basis that he could not believe that "in these days anyone would receive seventy-five cases of liquor and not take sufficient care to protect it." The more reasonable presumption was that he had ordered such an enormous amount of liquor in order to sell it. In these circumstances the magistrate was reluctant to give any leniency, "Prohibition doesn't prohibit," he lamented. "Fines don't seem to cut any figure these days. Jail is the only way, it seems." In addition to losing his cache of liquor, Katzman was sentenced to six months in reformatory or to pay an enormous fine of $1,000.

The sudden rise of rumrunning was creating an intolerable situation, at least according to the press. The *Star* featured numerous editorials decrying the situation and proclaiming that something must be done:

> The (liquor) traffic has been going on quite too long.
> The people who voted for temperance laws want to see
> those laws enforced. It is probable that no community
> in Canada has suffered more than the Border Cities
> from the epidemic of rum-running now upon us...
> every good citizen should demand the enforcement
> of the law.[15]

In a warning that would become all too prophetic, Magistrate Miers saw the situation as leading to escalating violence. "We must call a spade a spade... If conditions do not improve someone is going to be shot."

5

A LEADER FOUND

The summer of 1920 was one of remarkable opportunities for both Leslie Spracklin and Beverley Trumble. The Chappell House was filled with customers and making huge profits from Prohibition. On weekends, streetcars and taxis from Windsor brought in load after load of Detroiters who came to enjoy the offerings. And it was apparent from the crowds who exited the Chappell House that they were being served sterner stuff than coffee or tea. A few hotels still retained licenses to sell soft drinks and "near beer." However, the Chappell House had no license to serve any alcohol. It operated with impunity, and most of its clientele stumbled out of the roadhouse in a state of intoxication. A Toronto reporter described it offering "Whisky at fifty cents an inch in a little wine glass." The building itself was a rambling bungalow with rooms available upstairs, and downstairs "two large rooms, one with chairs and tables where the drinks are served, the other where dancing goes on to the accompaniment of a febrile piano." The Toronto reporter was shocked to see hundreds of men and women crammed into the Chappell House on the weekends enjoying themselves and laughing "at convention in oaths that would have made a mid-Victorian matron's hair turn grey."[1] Black waiters (almost the entire staff was black) quickly moved about the rooms taking orders and serving liquor and beer. For Babe Trumble, there was no need to engage in rum running. The Detroiters came to him, and he was more than willing to meet their needs. Still, he was surrounded by a coterie of hard men who undoubtedly kept him supplied and probably engaged in liquor sales across the border.

As for the Reverend J.O.L. Spracklin, he now found himself the head of a community church. Methodism in Sandwich had its origins in 1852 when the town became the head of the Wesleyan circuit known as the Sandwich and Windsor Mission. However, in April 1879, the Mill Street church was sold to the town and the focus of the Church in the area became Central Methodist in Windsor. It was not until 1904, that Methodist services were once again being held in private homes in Sandwich, and in 1907, a fine new structure was dedicated on Bedford Street. It was a small church, but beautifully encased in stained-glass windows. In March 1920, the *Border Cities Star* carried a full report on the "Popular Pastor" who had risen from being a machinist in an auto plant to a respected clergyman.[2]

By June 1920, the Border Cities seemed to have reached a crossroads. Rumrunning had ceased to be an occasional sport but was now emerging as a vast enterprise. The American Anti-Saloon League recognized the danger of the porous border and that in "cities situated like Detroit, officials of the organization say, a careful watch will be kept on the border. The Anti-Saloon league does not intend that Canada flood American communities with liquor..."[3] Despite these intentions, it would require a massive and costly police presence to actually enforce the law. Without such action, a tsunami of Canadian liquor across the border was inevitable. Respectable segments of society were openly alarmed about the situation. At the Essex County convention of the Women's Christian Temperance Union in June 1920, the ladies demanded that the law be enforced and that "drastic action be taken against boot-leggers." Essex County Baptists joined in a few days later with a resolution requesting the provincial government to take stern measures to enforce the *OTA*. The Baptists suggested that jail terms instead of fines was the only way to stop the law-breaking. The opinions of religious groups were bolstered by the *Border Cities Star*. W.F. Herman was a staunch Prohibition man and under his guidance, the newspaper became a dominant voice calling for enforcement of the temperance laws. Under an editorial banner "Enforce the Law," the *Star* suggested that "Every minister in Essex County should rise in his

This 1920s political cartoon pokes fun at the efforts to stop the flood of illegal booze coming across the border.

pulpit and condemn the wholesale bootlegging now in progress…"[4]

Yet, many in the Border Cities profoundly disagreed with the moralists and preachers. In June 1920, lawyer F.W. Wilson spoke to the Retail Merchants Association and vehemently denounced the *OTA*. In his view, the statute violated basic premises of British justice by denying trial by jury, by presuming an accused person's guilt, and requiring them to give evidence of their innocence. For example, section 83 assumed that an illegal sale of liquor had taken place in cases where there was no evidence of a sale. Section 88 provided that mere possession of liquor could be considered conclusive evidence that an offence was committed. As Wilson pointed out, it was a bad act which "leaves a magistrate free to presume a man's guilt." He gave the example of two men each having a gallon of whisky. Under the *OTA,* the magistrate could presume one man guilty yet free the other. Wilson concluded that "we have the law here but it certainly is not obeyed… Some of our best citizens seem to consider it no harm to break the act." Added to the controversy were comments from Michael Fallon, the Catholic Bishop of the Diocese of London which took in the parishes of the Border Cities. While he respected the law, Fallon opposed the *OTA* as being contrary to "British traditions of personal liberty as well as to the best Catholic traditions of personal responsibility." The principal spiritual leader of the Catholic residents of the border area had thereby openly diminished the law that many of them already held in disdain. As Father Beaudoin, the leading cleric among the French-Canadians of Windsor had counseled, it was temperate drinking, not prohibition, that was the goal. Perhaps it was about time to relax the morality laws that were increasingly controlling private lives. The progressive *Saturday Night* magazine suggested that the public was "getting a little fed up with the anti-horse race, anti-smoke, anti-drink, anti-anything movements."[5]

Even if they were outnumbered along the Detroit River border, the temperance faction had the law behind them, and it was a question of whether they could bring its power to bear. On June 11, Reverend H.A. Graham of Lincoln Road Methodist Church gave a sermon on the crisis. "These Border Cities have been specially besieged during the past four or five months by the forces of king Booze." Lawless elements from the countryside and especially from across the river in Detroit had "rallied to the standard of this inveterate enemy." What was desperately needed was a leader, "a wise man to unify and direct the forces that are logical and true…"

Saturday night, June 19, 1920 was similar to any other weekend revelry in the Border Cities, except that at one of the most boisterous of the roadhouses, the Chappell House, a Methodist minister was parked just outside the entrance. Spracklin had arrived there about 9:30 that evening, and counted from twenty-five to thirty cars parked around the tavern. The premises appeared to be filled to capacity and street cars and taxis were bringing new loads while spent revelers departed. They came in sober and inevitably departed drunk. And where were the police? As a matter of fact, Sandwich's chief of police, Alois Master, was sitting on the front porch of the Chappell House. One departing young lady was so intoxicated that she all but rolled off the porch. Another drunken girl actually perched on the chief's knee for a few moments to steady herself before he shooed her off. By 10:40, the chief entered the Chappell House for several minutes. Shortly after eleven, when Master emerged from the House, Spracklin sidled up to him and commented, "hello chief, some hell hole." Master replied, "Yes, its pretty loud tonight, but there's nothing we can do." Spracklin admitted his surprise that there was nothing he could do when so many people were obviously breaking the law right before his eyes. Shortly thereafter, Spracklin overheard the chief say to one of his constables that they were being watched by the preacher and a number of arrests were made.

The following Tuesday at the Sandwich town council meeting, Spracklin asked to address the council. "I come here," he solemnly began, "representing the law-abiding citizens of the town… Conditions at the present time in Sandwich are appalling and very little effort is being made to control them." He recounted his experiences of the preceding Saturday night as a witness to the horror that liquor was being openly sold in a roadhouse. Even worse, the police were quite aware of the situation and they all but condoned it. Spracklin concluded

Spracklin emerged into the public eye in 1920, with his first appearance before the Sandwich town council.

that Sandwich had become "a dumping ground for the lowest element…which comes to us from all parts of the United States to obtain what they are looking for-strong drink…There is a flagrant disregard for the law and so far the police have made no effective efforts to cope with the situation. The streets have become unsafe for our mothers, wives and daughters on account of the open debauch that is going on."

Chief Master was called forward to respond. Eighty years old, the police chief was a venerable figure whose time had passed. According to him, he had visited every hotel in the town on many occasions "and never yet saw a glass of liquor sold." His testimony was unconvincing, and several members of the council demanded an investigation. Mayor Ed Donnelly assured the citizens that something would be done. However, it became apparent after the council meeting that the mayor had no intention of doing anything. This was not surprising as there was so little to investigate. That bootlegging and illegal drinking was widespread and openly carried on along the border was hardly new. "There is nothing vague or mysterious about the situation," the *Star* noted. "Liquor is being brought in and sold in tremendous quantities."[6] In the lead editorial titled "Courageous Action," the newspaper praised Spracklin for his courage in bringing this situation forward, and that he "deserves the thanks of every law-abiding resident of the Border Cities."

Not everyone was so grateful. Mayor Donnelly, Babe Trumble, and Chief Master hired lawyers and threatened to sue Spracklin for libel. However, no pleadings were ever filed. According to Donnelly, the "downtowners" of Windsor should mind their own business and clean up their own city. Besides, Sandwich authorities were busy buying a new motorcycle to catch speeders. The mayor and councilors preferred admiring their new vehicle to spending time dealing with allegations of police corruption.

Yet the problem stubbornly refused to go away. At the end of June, one gang of bootleggers, thought to be Anderdon township farmers, engaged in a pitched battle near Amherstburg with a gang of town boys over the possession of a cache of liquor. A stock pile at the Indian burying grounds spurred the Amherstburg boys to stage the surprise raid. Before the conflict ended, over 300 shots were fired and three of the wounded were taken to hospital. It was, as the *Amherstburg Echo* noted, the largest battle fought in the area since the War of 1812. "That someone was not killed was a miracle of bad marksmanship and uncertain light."[7] And yet, this skirmish was only one example of the lawlessness that engaged the border, and demonstrated the increasing violence associated with the liquor trade. On July 30, five cars loaded with gunmen attacked the Tourangeau farm in Sandwich West in an attempt to steal liquor supplies. While they failed to get the goods they sought, they left the house riddled with bullets from high-caliber rifles. The situation seemed to be increasingly out of control, and yet no investigation was being convened in Sandwich. As Spracklin's frustration rose, he preached a sermon in which he chose a text from Proverbs which proclaimed that when the wicked are multiplied transgressions increase, but that "the righteous shall see their fall."[8]

At the Sandwich town council meeting of July 5, the Reverend appeared at the head of a delegation that demanded action. However, the members voted to silence Spracklin and Reeve Charles McKee, the chairman of the police committee, demanded that he submit his allegations in writing. One of Spracklin's allies, Councilor Pillon spoke up: "This thing is rotten. You don't have to go to the Chappell House to see it. It is at our doorsteps. I have seen conditions from my own home which is shocking." Nevertheless, the mayor ordered Spracklin to remain silent or be arrested. "You and the *Star* are not going to run this town" huffed Mayor Donnelly. "You've been doing a lot of squealing," he continued, and he thought that it was time to stop.

The Mayor had not reckoned with Spracklin. Astutely, the Minister sought out the support of Protestant churches along the Border Cities to his cause. A ministerial meeting held at All Saints' Anglican Church in Windsor united almost all of the major Protestant congregations behind Spracklin. John Coburn, the field secretary of evangelism and moral reform of the Methodist Council, assured "Mr. Spracklin that he had the hearty support of the department…it was unfair to expect Rev. Mr. Spracklin to carry on the fight single-handed…" There was no doubt that Spracklin had shone a light on a disturbing problem. Not only were local police indifferent to the lawlessness around them, in some cases, they were enthusiastic participants. On St. Patrick's Day 1920, one Windsor constable had willingly helped a bootlegger pile ninety-six cases of whisky in a truck and had then obligingly looked away as he drove off. The chairman of the Ontario License Board, J.D.

Flavelle, complained that the border police showed no desire to cooperate with his inspectors. The problem of police laxity was endemic up and down the Detroit River. At one point, Amherstburg had no police at all as the chief and constable were both fired. The only armed force remaining in town was the bootlegger collective, known as the "Blood and Thunder" gang. By mid-July, thirty-eight cases of whisky disappeared after being seized by Walkerville's police. They did not even bother to investigate and as a result, the entire Walkerville Police Commission was disbanded.[9]

Still, the Sandwich Council would not act. The issue finally came to a head a month after Spracklin's initial accusations. On Monday, July 19, Sandwich's Council convened and the town clerk read out Spracklin's indictment. This time the minister had broadened his accusations to include the police committee as also being hopelessly corrupt. It was nothing less than a declaration of war on the town's police and administration, an accusation of open neglect of duty. Mayor Donnelly hotly denied the allegations and asked what right Spracklin had to bring such charges: "I will put my reputation against his (Spracklin's) or anyone else's. I have known Spracklin since he was a boy and I am just as good as he is." At that point, the Reverend, who was under personal attack by the mayor, asked for a right to respond. Donnelly refused. According to the next day's account of the meeting, the minister called out:

Mr. Spracklin: But sir, may I speak?

Mayor Donnelly: Too much to do, out of order.

> Councilor Haggart, supported by Councilor Wright moved that Mr. Spracklin be given a hearing. The mayor refused to put the motion…
>
> Mr. Spracklin: Am I denied the right to address council?
>
> Mayor Donnelly: Out of order!

Again, Spracklin was refused an opportunity to present his case. The meeting broke up in chaos amidst cries for "Fair Play" and threats of beatings. After the council members departed, an unruly crowd gathered in the council chamber and threatened the minister. He in turn was being guarded by a phalanx of his partisans. One of his supporters called out to a reporter: "This man Spracklin has tonight lighted a torch which shall not die out until the whole province of Ontario is awakened to the conditions existing along the Essex border." In the meantime, the minister still had to get out of the Sandwich town hall in one piece.

Spracklin stood at the back of the hall as the mob surged around him, some shaking their fists at him and others hurling abuse. He called out in a voice trained to reach the far ends of a church: "I am not afraid of you; come on. I can use my fists if necessary."[10] Turning to a constable who offered to guard him, he said that would not be necessary. With a smile, he strolled through the hostile crowd to the front door and walked home alone. The next day's newspapers would refer to the Reverend J.O.L. Spracklin as "the fighting parson." A legend had begun and a leader had been found.

In July 1920, the *Christian Guardian*, the weekly of the Methodist church in Canada took up Spracklin's cause. This powerful, nationally distributed newspaper was appalled at the conditions he faced. "A fine moral sink-hole has been erected along the Canadian bank of the Detroit River...a nest of rumrunners and law breakers that pervades the district." But one Methodist clergyman had stood up to them and, as the *Guardian* phrased it, he was "putting up a splendid fight for decency and sobriety." The Toronto press, which rarely covered events south of Brantford, was amazed at what was going on along the border. From pitched battles near Amherstburg to high-speed boat chases along the Detroit River, Essex County had become a lawless, but nevertheless exciting, frontier. According to the *Toronto Evening Telegram*, "Nightly fights occur along the shore" on the forty-mile stretch of riverfront between Stoney Point and Amherstburg. Most of the rattle of gun fire was between rival rumrunning gangs attempting to steal each other's supplies. With only ten provincial inspectors on the border and the local police largely indifferent to bootlegging, the authorities were an insignificant presence. American police told the *Evening Telegram* that they were seizing 3,000 quarts a month, a figure they conceded was only a small fraction of the cross-border traffic.

Only days after Spracklin's denunciation, the *Evening Telegram* described to its readers how the borderlands had given in to a confluence of vices. In July 1920, the race tracks located just outside the city limits hosted a series of meets. The relatively small border communities featured three major tracks, a concentration far greater than that available in Toronto or Hamilton. This was no accident. With no tracks permitted in Michigan or Ohio, hundreds of gamblers eagerly crossed the border to take part in the two week-long race meets. On opening day, July 4, 20,000 punters, the vast majority of them Americans, jammed into the Devonshire Race Track just south of Windsor. It was the wildest and most exhilarating event hosted along the border, capturing the interest of everyone in the area. A Toronto reporter described how the usual price of fifty cents for a glass of whisky in a speakeasy went up to a dollar: "But the race mad mob cares little for money. So the Devonshire track meet is the underworld's harvest in more ways than one." He went on to describe this hellish revelry describing how "prostitutes swarm on the rail of the track 'talent'... as an additional insult of the decent element of Windsor."

With its convention of gamblers, drinkers, and whores, the race meet was an affront to Victorian

SIXTY ARRESTS OVER WEEK-END

Drunkenness, Gambling, and Disorderliness Rampant at the Border

This special dispatch to *The Globe* detailed the mischief along the Detroit-Windsor border in June 1920.

norms and was regularly condemned in Protestant church pulpits. Nevertheless, it was wildly popular and a profitable time for the riders, promoters, pickpockets, and horsemen (likely including Joseph Spracklin) who travelled the circuit. The culmination of the meet was the "Frontier Handicap" held in late July. While the meet was run before an enthusiastic, above-capacity crowd, to the *Evening Telegram* it was just another glance into the pit. Its reporter concluded that the Detroit River border had become "the plague spot of Canada."[11]

Plague or not, the scandals sold newspapers. The *Toronto Daily Star* sent down a reporter to monitor the bootleggers and describe the situation in the Border Cities. He found that not only was the shoreline poorly policed, it was composed of a maze of flats, lagoons, and small islands. The locals had an intimate knowledge of the easiest and most covert ways to cross the river. Everything in the area moved by boat, and not only were the provincials vastly out-manned, they did not even own a launch. The *Daily Star* reporter also visited the roadhouses, those dens of "open debauch" as Spracklin called them. Roadhouses such as the Chappell House were spaced along the river road, and in the nineteenth century had been refreshment stops for the stage coaches. Now they still served refreshments, but with their locations in the countryside they were safely removed from any police enforcement of the liquor laws. The goings-on at the roadhouses was all great fodder for the reading public of Toronto. According to the reporter, a night at a border roadhouse consisted of a "feverish orgy, undressed and unashamed, unbelievable if not actually seen." Having set that scene, the reporter described

The Sunnyside Hotel is pictured here in the late 1920s.

an evening at the Sunnyside Hotel in Sandwich West Township. There, men and women drank together in a well-appointed bungalow. Willow trees screened the verandah from the setting sun and "through the open windows came warm light and music and the sound of dancing feet." Young ladies and their escorts arrived for dinner and black waiters took orders for cocktails. While illegal, it was decidedly civilized and it hardly seemed the picture of a desperate public menace.[12]

Nevertheless, it had to be stopped. A few days after the Spracklin debacle at the town council meeting, the Toronto *Globe* demanded that the province's attorney general, William E. Raney, do something. "The reign of the whiskey-running outlawry in Essex county must be brought to an end" the *Globe* proclaimed. It suggested that the attorney general "dispatch a company of vigorous and vigilant officers to the district to effect a thorough clean-up." Essex County was not only a "disgrace," the *Globe* concluded that, "it has now become a menace."

Far cheaper than a company of police officers, however, was the one individual who had emerged as an enemy of the roadhouses and their trade.

Toronto was fascinated by the Reverend Spracklin, this man of the cloth who had alone stood up to the bootleggers. He was invited to the capital to meet with the individuals who would play the pivotal roles in Ontario's reaction to the liquor crisis. On Thursday, July 22, Spracklin met with Attorney General Raney and Liquor License Board Chairman, J.D. Flavelle. Nothing was released as to what was said at the meeting of the three men beyond a reassuring note that the situation was "well in hand." Chairman Flavelle was a Lindsay businessman, brother of the prominent industrialist Sir Joseph Flavelle, and a committed temperance man. However, in crafting the province's temperance enforcement policy he would be overshadowed by Attorney General W.E. Raney.

In photographs from the period, Raney presented himself as a dapper Toronto lawyer with a trim goatee and

an air of rectitude and confidence. Beginning his education in a log school house, Raney had gone on to earn a gold medal at Osgoode Hall and be called to the Ontario bar. Raney also crusaded on behalf of moral causes such as closing the race tracks. Firmly in the camp of moral reform,

William Edgar Raney, circa 1920.

he had first achieved notoriety through a series of essays condemning horse racing. When the United Farmers of Ontario unexpectedly won the 1919 election, they had to cast about for a legally trained individual to serve as attorney general. The UFO premier, E.C. Drury, settled on Raney, an urban lawyer with a mediocre record but a fixed moral compass, to spearhead the drive to enforce the temperance laws. Raney's appointment to the crucial post of attorney general would form part of Drury's plan to advance social reforms which included mothers' allowances, minimum wages for women, and especially a program to "uplift" the moral tone of Ontario. As historian Peter Oliver described them, the Drury men were "convinced that the great issues which confronted society would be resolved only through the creation of superior standards of personal morality."[13] Seen in this light, Drury's agenda was very much a continuation of the evangelical temperance crusade of the nineteenth century. Now that crusade was backed by the force of law.

The new attorney general faced an army of detractors. The *Toronto Evening Telegram* denounced him as "a moral reform bigot who will hasten to establish a reign of the saints."[14] But this was the man Drury wanted to turn the prohibition laws from pious aspirations into reality. One of the first problems confronting him was the fractious Detroit-Windsor border. On July 9, Raney made his first public pronouncement on the crisis in which he promised a total clean up. "Constitutional authority which seems to be fast disappearing must be re-established." He ordered commissioners to seize large liquor assignments and force the recipients to prove that they were intended solely for personal consumption.

It was apparent that the fines being handed out were merely the cost of doing business, and he wanted *OTA* offenders sent to prison. But above all, he needed a corps of vigorous police officers to start enforcing the law.

Raney was ignorant of, or perhaps just oblivious, to the fact that he was seeking to impose a law on a region that held it in disdain. What might have been acceptable, or even applauded, in Newmarket and Orangeville, was abhorrent in Essex County. A *Toronto Daily Star* reporter who spent several days in the region was shocked by what he found:

> The condition of the public mind in Sandwich west and the other districts is terribly demoralized. The people have no respect for the present liquor law or any other liquor law.
>
> The opinion of the majority of the public is that they are doing Canada a favor by carrying on this bootlegging as it brings in American money that would never otherwise come here.[15]

A Liquor Board official was astounded to learn that some of the most respected people in Essex County were participating in whisky running. Rumrunners had been found to include elected officials, policemen, and other prominent members of society. The distinctiveness of the border region, and its rejection of the laws restricting drinking, would not resonate with the attorney general. He was a man of fixed ideals, and all of Ontario would be treated as one. Every part of it would benefit from (or be subjected to) the laws of uplift. And he had just met with the man who personified exactly what he wanted done. The Reverend J.O.L. Spracklin mirrored the attorney general in his dedication to moral values and a determination to impose those values on anyone who resisted.

Meanwhile, back in Sandwich, it was apparent that those who favoured the easy-going ways of live and let live with the roadhouse operators were prevailing. Sandwich's police committee held their investigation on July 28 and only heard from police officers and Babe Trumble. For his part, Trumble seemed to relish the spotlight, and while he waited to testify, he freely gave the assembled reporters his opinion on current events. He thought that it was awful the way that Chief Master, "a fine old man," had been abused by the Windsor press. He went as far as to suggest that these accusations were part of a thinly disguised plot by Windsor and the *Border Cities Star* to initiate the annexation of Sandwich. Trumble admitted that while the Chappell House had previously had an unsavory reputation, he had cleaned it up and had even offered his boyhood chum Leslie Spracklin the chance to inspect the premises. He denied the charges, maintaining that "Liquor has never been sold in my house with my consent and I am prepared to deny that Mr. Spracklin saw the drunks coming out of my hotel as he said." Questioned about what kind of beer he would serve to a *Toronto Daily Star* (a heavily pro-*OTA* newspaper) reporter, Trumble replied "poison."[16]

The proceedings, including Trumble's testimony, were held in private and concluded after only half a day. Spracklin had already dismissed the investigation as "a joke" and refused to attend. Emerging from the conference room, Chief Master proclaimed: "It's all over. There was nothing against the police. Spracklin didn't even appear."

The war was far from over. On the day before the police committee meeting, Wednesday, July 27, Spracklin had been appointed a provincial license inspector by order-in-council. Official notification was on its way to Windsor but would not arrive until that Friday.

A few people had misgivings about this startling appointment. *The Port Hope Evening Guide* wondered about the propriety of a clergyman becoming an agent of the law, for perhaps the dignity of the Reverend's high calling was being diminished by his becoming an "official booze hunter." The *Border Cities Star* leapt to his defence and proclaimed, "It takes real courage, a high sense of duty and a spirit of genuine self sacrifice to do what Mr. Spracklin has been doing."[17] For its part, the *Christian Guardian* felt that it was about time for churchmen such as Spracklin to step forward. "The Methodist Church is a branch of the fighting forces of the Kingdom of God, our ministers are likely to be heard of every now and then from the heart of some nasty fight." Even as questions mounted on Spracklin's conduct almost all the provincial press would remain unwavering in their support.

In addition to appointing Spracklin, the attorney general issued a public statement:

Attorney General W.E. Raney has declared war on the rum-runners and bootleggers in the Windsor and

Essex districts and in co-operation with Hon. H.C. Nixon, provincial secretary, has started to clean up a situation that has been growing into a scandal and a disgrace. Law officers must now fight illegal liquor business as they might fight other crime, and local and provincial officers must chase down whiskey-runners as they would a murderer.[18]

This was a remarkable pronouncement. The *Ontario Temperance Act* was not a criminal law, nor a part of the *Canadian Criminal Code*. It was simply a provincial regulation on the same level as the *Municipal Affairs Act*. But Ontario's chief law enforcement officer was now dictating to his staff to treat infractions of the *OTA* as major criminal acts akin to murder.

Raney went on to explain that "the system has broken down in some of the border counties…" Some of this failure could be attributed to the division of enforcement between the provincial license inspectors who were under the control of the license board and the provincial police who were part of the attorney general's department. Local and provincial police officers were ordered by Raney to do their duty and cooperate with the license inspectors to enforce the *OTA*. To add further muscle, the total number of provincial officers on the border was increased from ten to fourteen. Shortly after Spracklin's appointment, Raney gave a speech in Erin, Ontario, in which he further refined his objectives. His speech identified the Border Cities as the main problem and claimed that "the geographic situation of Windsor, in conjunction with race track betting allowed under Dominion legislation, has made that city the greatest resort of gamblers and criminals on the North American continent." Even if the federal government refused to help, (Ottawa had advised Raney that federal police would not assist in enforcing provincial laws), and local police were less than enthusiastic, then the Province would see that the law was imposed on this unruly district. From now on, it was war on the bootleggers, and the attorney general's designated weapon on the Detroit River border would be the Reverend J.O.L. Spracklin.

6

INSPECTOR SPRACKLIN

S pracklin's first official day as a provincial license inspector ended in a brawl. On the Saturday after his appointment, he and two veteran inspectors raided three hotels. Unsurprisingly, they found liquor being sold at each establishment. Just outside Windsor, at Jackson's Corners, the inspectors forced their way into a room where the proprietor had protested that his wife was taking a bath. After breaking in, the inspectors discovered a bottle of whisky instead of a soaking spouse. An officer handed the bottle to Spracklin to hold as evidence. However, one of the occupants attacked Spracklin with a hammer, and he was barely rescued. Afterwards, Spracklin was modest about his initiation into the fight against rum running, but admitted that it was a "warm beginning."[1]

It was apparent that Spracklin could not accomplish his purpose alone and that other men accustomed to taking direct action were needed. How he made his selections is not known, but two of Spracklin's chosen men were the brothers Stanley and William Hallam. It is not surprising that the men he picked were tough, vigorous, and occasionally unpredictable. Once he had his "specials" sworn in by Crown Attorney Rodd as County Constables, a distinct force from the license inspectors who had previously been patrolling the border, the Fighting Parson was ready to take forceful measures. One thing was absolutely essential, and that was to get onto the river. Bootleggers had the finest speed boats available to them, and if the lawmen hoped to compete, they needed a fast boat. On August 26, Mousseau's men confiscated four rumrunning boats, including the Panther II. Having heard Spracklin's plea, Attorney General Raney put the Panther II at his disposal.

Spracklin and his men were now able to patrol the Detroit River and chase down suspected vessels who were shipping liquor to the United States. Apparently, he saw it as one of his prime duties to enforce the American Prohibition laws. On at least one occasion, his patrol boat was stationed at Belle Isle on the American side watching for Canadians landing with cases of whisky. He appeared oblivious to the fact that he had no legal authority outside of Ontario. But whatever he did, Spracklin knew that he had the provincial government and Toronto press squarely behind him.

In many ways, the ascendancy of rum running along the Detroit River was a godsend to the Toronto newspapers, and many of them sent reporters to cover the events. The *Toronto Evening Telegram*, a conservative, working-man's paper, had a staff reporter living in Windsor. He filed a dispatch of an interview with a former boxer, the "pocket Hercules"

Art Edmunds, who had served as a liquor inspector for two weeks. Despite Edmunds limited involvement, he became the *Toronto Evening Telegram's* principal source of information. Edmonds described the riverfront where former liquor caches, bottles, wires, and burnt-out cases littered the ground. When the inspectors tried to raid the Chappell House, they were outnumbered by the staff and beat a

J.O.L. Spracklin and his wife Myrtle are pictured here, circa 1920.

retreat. According to Edmunds, Mousseau's men were out-manned and out-gunned and not interested in taking risks. But none of the Toronto press could match the *Toronto Daily Star* for the depth and vitality of its coverage.

At the time of Spracklin's appointment, the newspaper glowingly described him as "Keen, practical, square, energetic, an athlete every inch of him, blazingly indignant at the drunken scenes of lawlessness he has been forced to witness…" Such an impressive specimen would no doubt work miracles in enforcing the temperance laws. And now that he was empowered by provincial sanction, the *Daily Star* imagined "his (Spracklin's) pastoral Ford working unflagging overtime…when he steps into the ring there will be a battle royal to the finish."[2] Joseph Atkinson, the publisher of the *Toronto Daily Star* sent a young reporter, Roy Greenaway, to cover the exploits of Spracklin's crew. As Atkinson was a fervent anti-liquor man, and a close friend of Attorney General Raney, there was no question that Greenaway's reports (if he wished to retain his job) would glorify the exploits of License Inspector Spracklin. Assigned to cover the action, Greenaway "lived with them (Spracklin's agents) and accompanied them on their raids…by day and night Spracklin struck on land and water." He recalled (many years later) that "Spracklin showed physical prowess that many a professional boxer might have envied. The hard-boiled pastor was soon hitting blows that really hurt."[3] In painfully florid prose, Greenaway described how Windsor bootleggers whispered the name of Spracklin "as did the English mother of that Black Douglas in the days of old 'Hush ye, hush ye, Spracklin will not get ye.'"

Reports from the *Toronto Daily Star* gave almost daily accounts of derring-do on the Detroit River border. The Reverend Spracklin was depicted as something of an action hero with his "huge frame, hardened by years of toil in a machine shop, lent itself admirably to the rough and tumble in fact too readily for his opponents." Greenaway supplied thrilling reports of this man of God confronting the liquor interests. Nor was the minister alone. He had gathered about him a group of like-minded heroes, and:

Neither threats nor rumors of threats however seem now to frighten the intrepid minister who, between making Leopard II (his latest patrol boat) ready for sustained action and breaking in a squad of exceptionally fine new officers, has very seldom in the last few days taken off his clothes and gone to bed.

At the end of October, Greenaway reported that "a certain Jew of Windsor" who, despite leaping over a fence "like a mad wild thing with the officers in hot pursuit," was apprehended by Spracklin and his men with a marked U.S. bill in his possession which proved that he had smuggled liquor across the border. Once again, no one questioned why Spracklin had inserted himself into an American case. In the same report, Greenaway recounted how the "Blood and Thunder Gang" had warned Spracklin and his men not to set foot in Amherstburg. These "whiskey desperadoes" were the worst sort, Greenaway assured his readers, and they meant business. "Tell them we are coming" was Spracklin's grim reply.[4]

Greenaway described one Halloween night when he and one of Spracklin's men tried to mount a watch on the Sunnyside Hotel. They were found out and retreated. Abandoning this position, they decided to stand guard over the Panther II. Sometime after midnight, they were awakened by shots being fired at the boat from a car. A few moments later, the same vehicle careened past the Spracklin manse and fired off a barrage of bullets into the residence. One shot barely missed Mrs. Spracklin.[5] Another just passed over the head of a former Sandwich special constable and now one of Spracklin's men, G.A. Jewell, who was guarding the premises. Yet, a gun barrage fired at the home and family of a law enforcement agent passed with only one brief report in the *Border Cities Star*.

While the local press seemed indifferent, if not increasingly irritated about Spracklin, one can only wonder what effect it was having on him. This assault was a personal violation, a demonstration that his enemies meant to harm not only him but his family. The mental impact on Spracklin must have been enormous when he started to realize the peril he had created for those around him.

At the same time that the *Toronto Daily Star* was printing almost daily accounts of these escapades, the local newspaper, the *Border Cities Star*, rarely mentioned Spracklin at all. Since his appointment as Inspector, he had almost disappeared from local view except when he blundered and filed the wrong papers in court or exceeded his jurisdiction. The reasons for the *Border Cities Star*'s indifference were apparent for even Spracklin complained that "Even the local papers have

This 1920 *Toronto Daily Star* cartoon depicts how both sides of the border were intent on stopping the cross-border liquor trade.

been thrown into line against them (his officers)... by the threat of the organized business men to withdraw enough advertising from them to put them out of commission."[6] The reality was that he was simply bad for business. So many businessmen in the Border Cities were now engaged in liquor transport in one way or another that Spracklin's antics had disrupted what was an enormously profitable enterprise at a time when the post-war economy was faltering and hundreds of veterans and their families were destitute. To many veterans, bootlegging offered the prospect of at least a little money and should be encouraged. A *Toronto Evening Telegram* reporter who was canvassing the shops of downtown Windsor was taken aback by the attitude at the border:

> This good natured toleration of the open violation of the Temperance Act has actually become a "state of mind" in the border cities.

By way of example, he cited an instance when he entered a cigar store and asked the owner, "What about this rum running stuff?" The owner replied, "My business was never better." When the reporter asked a druggist what he thought about the liquor traffic, he shrugged and responded: "Well, that's Detroit business" and as for his pharmacy business, it was "Fine, never better. That's the reason I have no time to bother about these newspaper reports of scraps on the river over so-called rum-running."[7]

The illegal liquor trade had become so vital to the local economy that at one point, Spracklin revealed that local business leaders had approached him and begged him to stop stirring up such adverse publicity. Thanks to the extravagant press reports resulting from Spracklin's raids, the Border Cities were becoming widely known as a bad place for business and a lawless refuge for bootleggers. Spracklin's response was that he had no interest in the local economy, but that he intended to fight not only the rum runners, but their agents who shipped alcohol from Montreal and the property managers who warehoused liquor. He would be unrelenting in his struggle against the "lawyers, brokers and real estate dealers" who made the liquor trade possible, and damn the consequences on those who made their living by it.

As he was so convinced that he was fighting God's battle, there would be no circumspection on Spracklin's part. It did not matter that he was impeding one of the largest and most profitable industries to emerge in the area. The transportation of liquor was becoming as important to local employment as the auto industry. As historian Philip Mason noted, in 1920 alone, 900,000 cases of whiskey were shipped into the Windsor area from Quebec, where most of them were sold in Michigan. Annual sales in 1920 totaled nearly "$219 million from Canadian whiskey and an additional $30 million from the sale of wine."[8] Aside from geography and location, the Detroit-Windsor borderland had many advantages that made it a prime spot for the new industry. First of all was supply. As Canadian laws permitted the personal consignment of whisky from outside the province to Ontario, it was quite legal for anyone to order hundreds of cases. A residence could be packed attic to basement with crates of liquor, ostensibly intended for the owner's consumption. As so frequently happened, these stocks disappeared with amazing speed and for reasons unconnected to the owner's thirst.

Added to this was another asymmetrical feature of border law. The manufacturing of liquor remained legal in Canada, so long as it was intended for export to another country or province. As a consequence, the Hiram Walker distillery remained in full operation throughout the 1920s, producing its famed Canadian Club whisky. This was an important factor, for unlike the diluted and dangerous products that came from hastily improvised American stills, the Canadian product was of known quality. "Canadians could rely on much higher quality equipment, professional

An alleged smuggling tunnel, more likely used for storage, under the Detroit River, circa 1920s.

workers, and experience to produce beverages, which were not only better tasting but also consistently free from poisonous substances, often a problem with unprofessional liquor production."[9] Moreover, the Hiram Walker distillery demonstrated a flair to adjust to the demands of Prohibition commerce. When bootleggers complained that the long-neck bottles of Canadian Club tended to break when transported in burlap bags, the Walker distillery obligingly switched over to a durable square "Gate Bottle" which could endure the rigours of bootlegging. For hundreds of men and women employed at the Walker distillery or playing a role in the transport across the Detroit River, the liquor business had become a way of life and a welcome means to support their families.

Those entering this new trade were not always the criminal low-lifes portrayed by the Toronto press. Many were leading citizens who could not resist the chance to make enormous profits. Typical of this group was Daniel Rocheleau, a former member of the Essex County Council, who was brought up on *OTA* charges in the summer of 1920. Rocheleau had bought sixty cases of whisky for $1,310. He sold them for eighty dollars apiece for a profit of $3,490, the average yearly wage of two workmen. Even the former mayor of Amherstburg was charged with rum running and offered the incredulous excuse that the liquor stored in his barn was there "in the public interest."[10] Many of those storing and then transporting liquor across the river were the farmers in the townships near Amherstburg. For many of them it was a once in a lifetime chance to make a lot of money. But Spracklin was indifferent to the facts of business.

He was also oblivious to the reality that by stopping some of the trade, and imperiling the remainder, he was making what did get through even more valuable.

It also became apparent shortly after his appointment that Spracklin had little knowledge of the law, or even of elementary policing. He misdated charges, which resulted in their being thrown out of court. On another occasion he arrested a man, took him to jail, and then released him on bail. One of the regular provincial inspectors pointed out to Magistrate Miers the next day that Spracklin had been doing this as a practice with no legal authority. Miers agreed and suggested that perhaps Spracklin and his men should be instructed as to the scope of their duties.[11] Frustratingly, they seemed to be beyond instruction. On October 1, one of the Hallam brothers arrested two suspected bootleggers who later turned out to be license officials. It soon became apparent that Spracklin's array of "exceptionally fine young officers" were little more than thugs. Stanley Hallam had recently worked for Inspector Mousseau but had been fired for the careless use of his firearm. It was later revealed that he had also served time in prison. The Hallams were rumoured to be heavy drinkers who could not leave a residence they were searching without helping themselves to a few valuables.

One evening the Reverend and the Hallams broke into the Dodlawn residence (without any warrant), scuffled with the couple, and arrested Mrs. Dodlawn. As she was sitting in the inspector's patrol car, a neighbour stepped in and told the Reverend that "she knew more about Spracklin than he would care to hear." Already there were awkward rumours circulating about the minister's personal conduct. Mrs. Dodlawn was released and returned to her house where her purse containing $100 had disappeared. In another instance, Spracklin and the Hallams arrested one Sauve and seized his car and fifteen cases of liquor. Afterwards, it was arranged that Sauve would pay the Hallams $1,400 to get back his car and to drop the charges. The Hallams, presumably, kept the liquor, as they did in the Poppet case where fifteen cases were seized and two kept for evidence. The Hallams sold the rest. Shortly thereafter, Inspector G.A. Jewell, another one of Spracklin's specials and an ex-convict who had been fired from the Sandwich police, raided the Dominion House (again without any search warrant) when the operators were absent. He confronted the persons present with a drawn revolver but eventually withdrew without taking any action.[12]

On September 17, in one of his most spectacular fiascos, Spracklin had used the patrol boat to follow a large yacht down the Detroit River and into Lake St. Clair. He had no reason whatsoever to believe that there was any liquor onboard the targeted vessel. Nevertheless, together with two other gun-brandishing officers, Spracklin boarded the ship and demanded that the occupants submit to a search. It turned out that the yacht was the private property of Oscar E. Fleming, Windsor's first mayor and one of its wealthiest and most influential citizens. At its masthead, Fleming's ship sported the blue ensign of the Royal Canadian Yacht Club, one of Canada's most elite clubs. At the time Spracklin and his men charged on board, Fleming's son was about to serve dinner to a number of distinguished ladies and gentlemen. They found their *soirée* rudely interrupted as gun-waving officers swarmed through the ship in search of alcohol. They found none. Oscar Fleming was outraged and demanded an apology. Spracklin refused, and Fleming filed a lawsuit.

Smashing in doors without warrants and demanding that the occupants explain themselves seemed to have become the preferred method of Spracklin and his men. The traditions of British law, wherein authorities had to have a properly issued search warrant to enter premises, seemed to the Reverend to be an unnecessary nuisance. Besides, he was empowered by a Higher Authority. Despite the mayhem he was leaving in his wake, there was no indication that Spracklin and his men had an appreciable effect in stopping or even slowing down the liquor trade. By late October, even the *Toronto Daily Star* conceded that the weekend along the Detroit River border was still "a grand carnival of booze." Hundreds of Americans were staggering off the ferry from Canada having consumed vast quantities of illegal liquor. All that Spracklin and his men had achieved was to infuriate the provincial liquor inspectors and local police who had been working on the border long before their arrival.

In fact, it was the constables of Ford City and two provincial police officers who took the fire in one of the bloodiest gun battles of the rumrunning era. The home of Frank Belleperche, at the then isolated corner of Tecumseh and Lauzon Roads, was attacked in mid-September 1920 by a gang of men who intended to make off with Belleperche's liquor stocks. At about one in the morning, three cars carrying the marauders pulled up by Belleperche's farmhouse. They cut his telephone wires, but neighbors reported to the police that an assault was imminent. The constables were called in to defend a cache of 200 cases that was undoubtedly intended to be sold at a later date. A Toronto *Globe* reporter covered the gun battle which see-sawed back and forth during the night and left Belleperche's house "riddled with bullets, blood spattered in his dooryard...a trail of blood leading to the cars and still more blood in the autos." The thieves gave up, drove off into the countryside, and abandoned their cars. Significantly, it was the local police, not Spracklin's specials, who stuck to their guns and drove off the bootleggers.[13]

The regular liquor inspectors had also been making major seizures of alcohol, usually more than Spracklin's crew. It was Mousseau's men who had tracked a huge shipment bound for five farmers in Sandwich West Township and seized over 1,000 cases. Between Mousseau's inspectors and the provincial police, ten carloads of liquor had been seized in 1920 and $260,000 in fines imposed. A parliamentary committee would hear how they had seized more liquor "than any others" and yet still commanded the respect of the community. It was this last aspect that troubled Inspector Mousseau. With their free-wheeling ways, Spracklin's men had tainted all law enforcement and made many citizens suspect that all liquor inspectors were criminals similar to the Hallams. By October 21, Mousseau had had enough. He telephoned License Board Chairman Flavelle, gave him a detailed account of how Spracklin and the Hallam brothers had been breaching civil rights, and demanded that unless they were removed, he would resign his position as head of the department in Essex County. Mousseau further contacted the press and told them that he was fed up with giving "free lances" legal authority to do as they pleased.[14]

Meanwhile, Attorney General Raney was already under growing pressure to hold public hearings into the crisis along the Detroit River. And it was a crisis. Magistrate Alfred Miers, who had been working at an unrelenting pace trying to keep up with *OTA* cases, reached the limit of his endurance by the end of September. Hearing a case against Oliver Grandmaison, a respected farmer with a large family, Miers adamantly refused to implement Raney's directions that all bootleggers be sent to jail on their first offence. This was not justice, nor should judicial officers be directed on how to hand out sentences. It had reached a point where the temperance law was not respected by any level of society. "Prohibition has been tried and is a failure," Miers was reported to have said, "I don't believe the liquor traffic can be done away with by law." For this, he was harshly rebuked by no less an authority than the Toronto *Globe*. It held that if that is what this Magistrate thought, then "The bench is no place for him... Such Magistrates are not of the caliber needed today along the border. They should be removed without a moment's hesitation."[15] Days later, Miers was called before the attorney general to explain himself. He denied saying that Prohibition was a failure, but pointed out that with the flood of liquor being delivered to Essex County, it was apparent to all that Prohibition did not prohibit. Four weeks later, Magistrate Miers collapsed and died. He had just turned fifty.

By late October 1920, the situation was clearly spinning out of control. Those who defied the law seemed to have the upper hand, while law enforcement was divided among itself. The authorities were becoming anxious, and on October 21, the *Border Cities Star* reported that Spracklin and his men had been cleared of blame by Commissioner Flavelle. Up until this time, no one had known anything about any official complaints or the nature of the alleged infractions. Now it was revealed that he had been cleared before it had ever been announced that he was under suspicion. The only thing publicly reported was that Spracklin had been vindicated and that he and his men were returned to duty. It was all very mysterious. A few days later, during an interview with *Toronto Daily Star* reporter Greenaway, Spracklin sounded a note of abandonment. He recognized that he had lost popular support and that the local press and business community were now lining up against him. The "liquormen" had their sympathizers, including "some of the most important men here" who were "trying to frame up and publish every discrediting thing, even absolute falsehoods against us." Spracklin admitted that there was nothing for it but a full public inquiry or a trial.[16]

The pressure for an investigation into Spracklin's conduct was mounting, and some of it was coming from an unexpected source. James C. Tolmie, the Member of the Provincial Parliament for Windsor, was one of the most prominent anti-liquor men in the Ontario Assembly. But even he was not oblivious to the rising discontent against Spracklin and his agents. Tolmie had been the popular Minister of St. Andrew's Presbyterian Church since 1894 and had run as an "abolish the bar" Liberal in 1914. Due to a split in the local Conservative ranks, the pro-temperance Tolmie carried what was probably one of the wettest constituencies in Ontario. In the 1919 election, he became more circumspect and refused to endorse the pro-temperance referendum. His flexibility earned him re-election. Now, Tolmie was being bombarded with affidavits from persons victimized by the specials. Windsor taxicab drivers had been an especially profitable target for the Hallam brothers. It was nothing to them to get into a cab, indicate to the cabbie that they could be charged with transporting liquor, and demand a payment to forgo laying charges. Most drivers knew that under the provisions of the *OTA* their guilt would be presumed, so they paid.[17]

It seemed to Spracklin's men that the ordinary laws simply did not apply to them. The growing anger against this unbridled breach of civil liberties and legally sanctioned extortion was creating a furor across the Border Cities. By late September, the pressure was irresistible, and a special committee of the legislature, with J.C. Tolmie one of the leading members, was formed to examine the operation of the *Ontario Temperance Act*. In theory, the committee was directed to investigate enforcement across the province, but everyone knew that its focus would be on the crisis at the Border Cities.

7

"THIS MAN SPRACKLIN
IS A FOOL"

The accusations against Spracklin and his men were mounting and could no longer be ignored. Stanley Hallam took it upon himself to stop a funeral procession and search a hearse to see if there was any concealed alcohol. This was too much, even for Toronto, and on October 21, Provincial License Commissioner J.D. Flavelle ordered Spracklin to fire him. His brother William had already left Windsor and was living in Toronto. But Methodist reinforcements were on the way. The specials were shored up by Spracklin's brother, the Reverend Arthur Spracklin of Malden and Mark Heaton, a farmer and county constable. Neither man had any police training. Days after they signed on, both Arthur Spracklin and Heaton engaged in a heavy exchange of gun fire with a supposed bootlegger's vehicle. Young Arthur would quickly live up to the family's reputation. A few days after his appointment, he and another officer stopped the car of two of Essex County's most prominent citizens: W.L. Messenger, the manager of Windsor Postum Cereal, and Reeve C.C. Chauvin of Sandwich West. When Arthur pulled out his gun and announced that he would search the vehicle, Messenger protested that he was no bootlegger and that Arthur had no right to go through his car. He was promptly handcuffed. Both Messenger and Chauvin wrote to Attorney General Raney and promised that lawsuits would follow.[1]

The number of accusations and the accumulation of affidavits documenting Spracklin's abuse of authority could no longer be overlooked by Toronto. When the special committee on the *Ontario Temperance Act* convened in the Reception Room at the Ontario Parliament Buildings on September 28, Flavelle was put to the test as to how he had been enforcing the Act. He immediately laid the blame on the asymmetrical system of laws that governed the Detroit-Windsor border. While the United States had absolute Prohibition, in Canada a person could stock up on as much alcohol as they pleased for their own use. Naturally enough, many persons were selling their supplies, and the sale of these stocks of liquor had become big business. Flavelle noted that "in Windsor we have had men fined as high as $2,000, and they went away smiling, saying that they had made five or six thousand dollars out of the transaction." He explained to the committee members that while it was one thing to enact temperance legislation, that enforcement was entirely different. He gave the example of railway workers. These men normally worked for $200 or $300 a month. A bootlegger who sought to get an entire rail car of illegal alcohol across the border would offer them $5,000 or $10,000 to oversee the shipment. It was a huge, overwhelming temptation for most railway men. As for the bootlegger, he stood to make a fortune of $60,000 or $100,000 if the shipment crossed the border. When adjusted for inflation, a single rail shipment could bring in millions of dollars. Policing this situation was especially difficult, and Flavelle noted that few inspectors had been assigned to the border in early 1920. Now there were sixteen or seventeen inspectors and Ontario Provincial Police working on liquor enforcement who had confiscated over $250,000 in contraband stock. In contrast, the thirty-eight local police had only seized $14,000. "They were doing practically nothing" he concluded.[2]

The committee chairman and Provincial Secretary, Harry Nixon, was satisfied that at least outside of the Border Cities the temperance laws were being enforced. However, at the subsequent committee meetings, the cracks in the system began to show. Windsor's J.C. Tolmie questioned Flavelle on just where he was getting some of the inspectors. One of the Hallams had a prison record and the background of the rest was questionable. Was there not "a danger of bringing the whole Act into disrepute in the possibility of having men of that character working for the Board?" W.S. Dingman, the Vice-Chairman of the License Board, explained that in Windsor, the inspectors had to cope with a unique situation. The border was lined by "a number of very disreputable road houses up and down the river." Even though the licenses had been taken away from many of these establishments during the war, the owners retained a clientele and continued to operate illegally. With regard to assisting enforcement of the *OTA*, "There is a great deal of lack of sympathy in Windsor even among the well-to-do and respectable people." In such a defiant place, drastic measures were required.

On November 2, the committee heard from Windsor lawyer A.F. Healy. One of the city's most respected citizens, Healy had practiced law in Windsor for fifteen years and was a former president of the Chamber of Commerce and a member of the Utilities Commission. He had come of his own volition to Toronto to tell the committee that the real situation along the Detroit-Windsor border was far different from that being daily portrayed by provincial officials, or in the sensational accounts found in the *Toronto Daily Star.* Healy began by praising License Inspector Mousseau, who had been on the job for years,

Some of Spracklin's squad of "specials," 1920. From left to right are: P.A. Clarke, Reverend Arthur Spracklin, Frank Bell, John Bell, and Thomas Eades.

as a man of the "highest caliber, but absolutely without competent help." Mousseau and the Ontario Provincial Police had been bearing the load in enforcing the *OTA* and had laid 803 criminal charges, collected $260,000 in fines, and seized ten carloads of liquor. In so doing, these trained police officers had still retained the respect of their community. In contrast, the recently appointed Spracklin had surrounded himself with men of morally dubious character. One of his specials, G.A. Jewell, was an ex-convict who had been fired from the Sandwich police for taking money from a prisoner. Without a warrant, Jewell and a fellow special broke into the house of the White family and held Mrs. White at gunpoint as she held her little girl in her arms. From the Hallams stealing Mrs. Dodlawn's purse during a warrantless search to planting evidence to substantiate a charge, the special agents seemed to know no law other than their own.

Nothing was sacred to Spracklin. Only the previous Sunday, his men had stopped vehicles leaving Assumption Church after Mass. Fifteen cars were searched without any warrants or probable cause. One of the regular license inspectors witnessed the spectacle and warned Spracklin's specials: "You are going too far, this is an outrage." According to Healy, the amount of bribes paid to the specials came to $7,500, and these included only the cases where the victims were willing to come forward. The amount of liquor seized by the special officers and resold by them could run as high as $75,000. "I think it is wrong that in our community people, some of whom are poor and have no remedy, that these men should be allowed to prey on them with guns and without warrants." Forbes Godfrey, a Conservative member from York West, called out, "Hear, hear." Healy questioned why the Hallam brothers had simply been dismissed when they should be facing criminal charges. Was there no accountability? He begged the committee to recommend that only properly trained officers be appointed, and that a competent judge be authorized to look into the accusations against Spracklin and his men. Forbes Godfrey interjected, "This man Spracklin is a fool based on that," to which Healy responded, "Why should the government appoint fools to enforce the law?"

After this testimony, Raney attempted to minimize the damage and suggested that Healy's comments were merely his impressions. Healy retorted that the accusations were a matter of record and that an investigating judge could determine their reliability:

> To put it briefly, we feel that the department have sent up a lot of men with no past records, their records never having been investigated; they arm them: they give them blank search warrants to break into homes and they have terrified our community. We will not stand for it.[3]

J.W. Curry, a Liberal member of the committee from Toronto and a lawyer who had served as a Crown Attorney for fourteen years, was aghast at Healy's assertions that Spracklin had made it his practice to carry a sheaf of blank search warrants with him and insert a name and address whenever he felt like going through a premises. "No department can give anybody authority to use blank search warrants," Curry observed, incredulously. Healy replied, "It is being done in our community."

On the following day, Spracklin was summoned to Toronto to respond to Healy's charges. But instead of directly addressing them, he launched into a recital of how he became a liquor inspector. Before his appointment, Sandwich was the site of public drunkenness, fights, and racing cars, enough "to make any man's blood boil." Spracklin's was certainly past the boiling point. He became an inspector, and with him, ten other Ontario Provincial Police were sent to the border. Many of them proved unable to resist temptation and they had been found drunk on duty or accepting bribes. Not Spracklin and his men, for his special squad of county constables were made of sterner stuff. During his testimony, he denied Healy's allegations that his men were seizing and reselling liquor. With regard to the warrantless searches, he knew that Inspector Mousseau also used blank search warrants. What could they do? If a squad came across a hundred cases of whisky stored in a cottage there was no time to drive downtown and get a warrant. Such a delay would only enable the bootleggers to move liquor across the border. One member responded: "That is where we want it, out of Canada."

The rest of the committee pooh-poohed these comments, and they were almost fawning in their attentions towards Spracklin. After all, he was the darling of the Toronto press, the dauntless foe of the bootleggers, and he was doing this at great risk to himself and his family. Admittedly his was risky work, and when one MPP asked Spracklin if he carried a gun, he responded that he did. The member then enquired if he was presently carrying one. There must have been a collective intake of breath when Spracklin confirmed that he was armed. He was sitting at the committee table with a loaded handgun. Why he, or anyone, would feel the need to carry a weapon into the provincial parliamentary committee seemed extraordinary. It might perhaps be explained by the fact that he had been carrying a gun for weeks, and that he had been regularly exchanging fire with bootleggers. Perhaps his caution was understandable, but carrying a loaded weapon into Parliament should have given pause that this man was on a dangerous mental edge.

Inspector M.N. Mousseau followed him and explained that Spracklin's men and his own often came into conflict when they were pursuing the same bootleggers. Not only were they working at cross-purposes, the specials so frequently resorted to their firearms that the regular officers refused to accompany them. When asked if he had a gun, Mousseau replied that he did not. He had never seen the need to go about armed. Forbes Godfrey muttered that in that case "you haven't got much publicity." Mousseau replied "I don't want publicity at all." When committee members grilled Mousseau on conditions in Essex,

'FULL CONTROL OR I RESIGN,' M.N. MOUSSEAU

Chief Inspector Appears Before O.T.A. Committee

"All I Want Is Your Confidence," Say Spracklin

Liquor inspectors M.N. Mousseau and Spracklin are at odds during their appearances before the O.T.A. committee.

he tried to explain to them that circumstances were different from the rest of the province. One thing that had shocked him was that "I found so many reputable farmers, men of good character heretofore, right in this business." Some of the members were aghast. Surely, anyone in the rumrunning trade must be a thug or gangster. Mousseau corrected them and explained that in Essex most people did not consider the trade particularly heinous, and many respectable members of the community participated in it. Commissioner Flavelle sensed an opportunity to defend Spracklin and interjected that "extreme measures have been demanded by extreme conditions." Flavelle then launched into an extended paean to Spracklin, who was "a vigorous young man" who had "accomplished a great deal of good in checking the traffic very very materially." He dismissed Mousseau, who was several years older than Spracklin, as a "polished French gentleman."[4]

However, the day did not end with this rousing endorsement. Provincial Police Superintendant Joseph E. Rogers was the final witness called before the committee. Rogers, already a legendary figure in police circles, had been the province's second detective in 1884 and was one of three detectives who founded the Criminal Investigation Branch in 1897. When the Ontario Provincial Police was created in 1909, he became Superintendant. Rogers was blunt in his assessment of the enforcement of the *OTA*. He was quite aware that the roadhouses along the border were breaking the law and selling real beer and liquor, but he wondered whether anything could really be done to stop them. When he was asked if liquor enforcement could be made part of the duties of local law enforcement, he was unequivocal: "Absolutely no. It cannot be done." When asked why, he explained that "the public generally have respect for the law… You go looking for information in connection with liquor, however, they will not give it to you." When people did not respect a law, they would not help the police to enforce it, they "won't inform on their neighbors, ordinary folk would not be spotters." With regard to the Reverend Spracklin and his men, Rogers was firm: "my men…they would not work with the Hallams."[5]

The pro-temperance press put the best spin they could on these events. The Toronto *Globe* (which had all but buried Healy's accusations) carried an editorial that heaped praise on Spracklin: "Since Mr. Spracklin assumed his duties he has been a terror to the rum-runners and has cut off a large part of their business."[6] But as the committee adjourned on the late afternoon of November 3, it was apparent that further proceedings, and quite likely a full judicial inquiry, would follow. At any future inquiry the full extent of the breaches of civil liberties, not to mention the outright extortion and thefts committed by Spracklin's special agents, would inevitably come out. The opposition in Queen's Park would roast the premier and his attorney general for having created such a debacle. Spracklin's appointment, which only three months previously had seemed such a grand gesture, was now turning into a political nightmare. Criminal charges were likely, and Raney, as Spracklin's sponsor, would bear the full brunt of the responsibility for his appointment. It is not known what Raney thought of his predicament, or how he imagined he could survive it.

He could have had no premonition that in just over forty-eight hours Spracklin would commit his most dramatic act yet. It would be such a violent deed that it completely overshadowed everything else he had done in the past three months. The aftermath would obliterate interest in lesser charges and in the process redeeming Spracklin's patron.

8

BLOODY MADNESS

F riday nights in the Border Cities were rarely sedate affairs. On November 5, the Empire Theatre was showing *The White Moll* staring Pearl White. It was a sizzling production in which the lead actress portrayed a woman whose "one thought was to destroy- to plunder- she went too far." For those who genuinely wanted to go too far, there was a wide array of blind pigs selling alcohol not far from the ferry stop from Detroit. And for those who were willing to venture farther out, the roadhouses offered dancing, music, and, invariably, illegal liquor.

Just back from Toronto, Spracklin had been patrolling the streets of Windsor and Sandwich that Friday night and had returned home early in the evening. Several times during the course of his patrols he had driven past the Chappell House without incident. Early on Saturday morning, he received an urgent call and was again on the streets with four of his specials: Heaton, the brothers Fred and John Bell, and T. S. Eades. At about 2:30 a.m., they noticed something peculiar and stopped in front to the Chappell House. According to Spracklin's later account, he saw lights on in the lower floor of the hotel and a badly injured man lying on the ground just outside. When Spracklin got out to attend to him, he recognized the man as Ernest Deslippe. He asked "Hello Ernie, what's the matter?" to which he replied, "Oh, I got knocked out." Another figure stood in the dark behind Deslippe who Spracklin recognized as Beverley Trumble. "Hello Bev," he said to the man he had known since boyhood. "Hello Les," Trumble replied. Spracklin then asked what had happened, to which Trumble responded that it was no big thing.

Helping Deslippe to his feet, Spracklin carried him over to a street light to get a better look at his wounds. Spracklin had no misgivings that Deslippe was a bootlegger and may have come to grief at the hands of some of his colleagues. "This is too darn bad, Ernie," he said, "some of your own bunch may have beaten you up. No matter how hard I fight you, as an officer, this is a dirty shame." After their brief talk, Spracklin was joined by his men. Babe Trumble was no longer to be found. As he later recounted, Spracklin called out, "Come on squad, and we all went to the hotel. We rapped at the front door and said, 'Open up boys, provincial officers.'" There was a short man on the inside with a gun who merely laughed. There were seven or eight men inside and one called out, "You can't get in."

While they had come across the injured Deslippe, there was no indication that there was any transport, sale, or consumption of illegal liquor going on inside the Chappell House. Nevertheless, Spracklin was determined to get in. The specials slipped open a side window, and Spracklin proceeded to the barroom to see if he could find any contraband. He came face to face with a Detroit bootlegger, William Morton, and several others from Trumble's entourage. Spracklin castigated him for beating Deslippe: "I fight you fellows pretty hard, but it's a fright for you to beat your own men up." Morton replied that everything was in hand and that they would look after Deslippe. At that point, Spracklin made his way around the crowd of men and went behind the bar area in search of liquor. One of Trumble's men came up to Spracklin and announced that he had not seen him since school days and asked to shake his hand. With some hesitation, Spracklin did so.

Moments later, the swinging doors leading into the kitchen burst open and a voice shouted: "Let me see your badges, every one of you. I'll shoot every damn one of you if you don't show them to me." Emerging from behind the bar, Spracklin saw Babe Trumble waving a cocked gun in the direction of the specials. Spracklin ran into the kitchen and pulled out his automatic pistol. Behind him, Constable Mark Heaton also burst in and knocked Trumble's arm upwards. Spracklin recalled, "I saw Trumble's gun swing on Heaton. I said to myself, there goes Heaton. It was a question to me whether or not I should shoot first to save my officer." However, instead of focusing on Heaton, Trumble advanced on the specials who retreated before him. "Back off boys," Spracklin called out. "We don't want any trouble." As the officers backed away, for the first time, Trumble noticed Spracklin. He confronted him and said, "Damn you Spracklin, I am going to shoot you," and pushed a gun into his stomach. According to Spracklin, he "hesitated for a few seconds," and then decided "it was either him or me." He fired a shot point blank into Babe Trumble's abdomen.

After firing, Spracklin shouted, "Back squad" and he and his men quickly left the building. None of them considered preserving any evidence. No one seized the gun that Trumble had been waving, and none of the specials bothered to render any assistance to the man who had just been shot. Several hours after the incident, Patrolman Benjamin Snider of the Sandwich force searched the Chappell House looking for a revolver, but found nothing. After making sure that his men were safe, Spracklin drove to Windsor and surrendered himself to the police. With no small understatement, he told the desk staff: "I have got into a little trouble gentlemen." Instead of being locked up like a common criminal, he was simply placed in a detention room. Neither was his name entered on the police blotter. It was one of the first indications that the Reverend Spracklin was above ordinary treatment. The Windsor Police Chief ordered that cordons of officers surround the station in case a bootlegger gang sought revenge. But as a cold, foggy dawn broke on November 6, it was apparent that nothing was going to happen, and the officers were dismissed back to their beats.[1]

Back at the Chappell House, the wounded Trumble had stumbled into the arms of one of the House's regulars, Ed Smith. Trumble's wife, Lulu, appeared and together they dragged him into the living room. Most of his clothes were stripped off and he was bleeding profusely. Doctors were summoned but nothing could be done to stop the bleeding. Dr. W.G. Beasley found Trumble unconscious on the floor, his head supported by Smith. Babe was pale, breathing slowly, and his pulse was slow. In twenty minutes, Babe Trumble was dead.

The *Toronto Globe* reported "Feeling ran high throughout the border cities last night, and police said they had heard open threats to 'shoot Spracklin on sight.'" After Trumble's body was removed to the Janisse funeral home, the county coroner, J.S. LaBelle, was contacted. Events now fell under the control of the Essex County Crown Attorney, John H. Rodd. Always active in local politics and the Liberal party, Rodd had been Crown Attorney since November 1904. An unflinching enforcer of the moral laws, he insured that prize fighting matches were banned and woe to any group of youngsters who tried to play baseball on Sunday. Rodd was also a prominent member of the Methodist Church and a staunch temperance advocate. Under the UFO government, Rodd had been directed to get the local police on board with enforcing the liquor laws. At the same time as Spracklin was appointed, Rodd was being instructed by Raney to take "charge of the campaign

The *Border Cities Star* banner headline announcing Trumble's death on November 6, 1920.

against the bootleggers."[2] In so doing, Rodd would often have contact with Inspector Spracklin as they tried to coordinate their objectives. It was apparent that so far as the Reverend Spracklin was concerned, Rodd could hardly be considered neutral.

On the same day of the killing, an inquest was hastily convened to examine what had occurred. Spracklin's lawyer, R.H. Brackin of Chatham, demanded that a full panel of twelve (instead of the usual eight) jury members be selected. As a result, it was not until nine that evening that Coroner J.S. LaBelle convened the inquest at the Sandwich Courthouse. The atmosphere was electric, and the police carefully searched every person entering the courtroom. There were no empty seats available. A gasp came from the crowd as the first witness took the stand. It was Lulu Bell Trumble, wearing a black silk dress and an expensive Hudson seal coat, topped by a bird of paradise hat. Her four-year-old son, Lester, and twenty-month-old Robert accompanied her. Lulu recounted how she had been sick that evening, and that her husband was in her room filling a hot water bottle. They could hear noises downstairs and heard a knock and a demand to see Mr. Trumble. Babe put down the water bottle and rushed down to the lower level. Lulu followed and heard her husband call out to someone, "What is the idea?" At first she had not recognized Spracklin, but then she noticed him standing in the kitchen doorway. She heard Spracklin reply, "We want to go through the house." Trumble asked, "Then why the guns? You never were refused admittance. Who are these other men and how did they get in?" He then demanded to see their badges to prove that they were officers. As he walked towards Spracklin, Lulu heard a gunshot "and that is the last I remember except that Beverley cried, 'You dog, you've shot me.'"[3]

According to her, Spracklin stood still, stunned by what he had just done. Abruptly, he and his men turned around and disappeared through an opened window. With the help of Ed Smith, Lulu carried her husband into the bedroom where he died a few minutes later. She denied that he had been carrying a weapon of any sort. The only things in his hand were a hot water bottle and a cigarette.

For 3 a.m., there seemed to be an unusual number of men and women out and about on the ground floor of the Chappell House. Several of Trumble's men gave their stories. Basil "Jack" Bannon heard Trumble call out several times "have you a warrant?" While he did not witness the shooting, Bannon saw a mortally wounded Trumble stagger towards his apartment moments later and calling out "I am shot." Bannon testified that "I saw no gun. I never saw Trumble with a gun." Another bystander, Stephen Wallace, interestingly enough a Canadian Pacific Railway switchman, recalled hearing Trumble call out loudly three times, "Have you a warrant?" Then he heard the shot. Two women who were casually lounging at a table were not called to testify.

Spracklin's men all gave accounts that supported their chief's version. Finding the front door barred, they had forced open the dining room window to gain entrance and drew their weapons. According to Mark Heaton, once it appeared that the men in the bar would not resist, he put his revolver away. However, moments later Beverley Trumble appeared flashing a gun in the faces of the officers and demanding to know what they were doing in his house. Heaton tried to grab his weapon but was dragged back. He heard but did not witness the shooting. Another officer, Frank Bell, was confronted by Trumble who waved a gun in his face and demanded to see his badge. Bell produced it and Trumble backed him up towards the door. Bell then heard Trumble call out "damn you Spracklin, I'll shoot you." Seconds later he heard the shot. Spracklin recounted the incident consistent with the statement that he had made to the Windsor police. Trumble had confronted him with a curse and a promise to shoot. Spracklin described what happened next:

> I hesitated for a few seconds. I do not know how long. It seemed like hours to me, as it always does under such circumstances. It came to my mind that it was either him or me. But I even then waited some seconds, hesitating to protect my own life.
>
> Then I fired.

Spracklin seemed intent on not only describing the incident, but providing an explanation for his motives. "It was simply life for me, or life for him."

Dr. W.C. Pepin had conducted the post-mortem and concluded that the shot had severed the victim's femoral artery and that he had died of internal bleeding. The inquest had been in session for three hours, and it was just after midnight, the beginning of the Lord's Day. Not only was it inappropriate to have judicial proceedings on a Sunday, the most crucial figure in the inquest was absent. Ed Smith, the man who had been standing directly behind Trumble when the shot was fired, could not be found. The inquest was adjourned to the following Monday.

The reaction across Ontario reflected the shock that a Methodist minister, in the act of enforcing the temperance laws, had shot down and killed a man. The

POLICE FEAR ATTACK ON ONTARIO PASTOR

Authorities Spirit Away Man Held for Killing Innkeeper to Jail at Sandwich.

HIS PLEA IS SELF-DEFENSE

Inquest Is Adjourned to Search for " Ed Smith," Who Is Said to Have Seen Shooting.

Even the *New York Times* covered the Spracklin inquest, as seen in this article from November 7, 1920. However, Spracklin was "spirited away" to Chatham, not a jail in Sandwich.

Toronto Daily Star rallied to Spracklin's cause. Trumble was obviously a criminal and the real crime was the failure of the Border Cities people to rally to the Reverend's assistance. "Mr. Spracklin has been engaged in a difficult and dangerous task," the article claimed the magnitude of which should have required more resources. To the *Hamilton Spectator*, there was no doubt of his innocence, for the Reverend "had good reasons for fearing that he was the object of hatred by many desperate men." If anything, it was Spracklin who was the victim, for the killing had (as the *Peterborough Examiner* concluded) "involved in a serious predicament a man who had the courage of his convictions."[4] Methodist wagons were circled in defence of one of their own, and the day after the shooting, Sandwich Methodist Church raised $10,000 for Spracklin's defence fund. Reverend H.W. Crews of Central Methodist Church in Windsor spoke out strongly on Spracklin's behalf. There was no question that he should continue in the Church for "We do not unfrock Methodist ministers for fighting the whisky trade." In Detroit, George Gullen, the pastor of Grand Boulevard Methodist, castigated those Detroit businessmen who boasted of their patronizing the Chappell House. "I have heard them call Beverley Trumble a good fellow," Gullen said, the implication being that Trumble got what he deserved.[5]

Across Ontario, the reaction was much the same. The London Methodist Conference was solidly behind the fighting parson and wished to "place on record our warmest commendation of the active and effective campaign." The powerful *Christian Guardian* declared that the enforcement of the prohibition laws was more

This photograph from November 8, 1920, was captioned "Sandwich minister on return from Chatham." From left to right are P.J. Clark, Reverend Spracklin, Duncan McNabb, and Frank Bell.

important than "any merely sentimental feeling stirred up by the thought of taking human life." There was a vital principle at stake, "Respect for the law must be re-established, and its right vindicated, no matter at what cost, even indeed at the cost of human life, if it has to be."[6]

Windsor police felt uneasy at holding a minister in jail during a Sunday. Consequently, he was granted the privilege no other prisoner in his place would get, to be set at liberty until the inquest resumed. Detective Duncan McNabb of the Windsor police accompanied Spracklin to Chatham. There he was well received; he attended church services and held an informal reception attended by many prominent Kent County Methodists. Also paying court to him in Chatham was the Chief License Officer of Ontario, the Reverend J.A. Ayearst. A fellow Methodist minister, Ayearst was also using his public office to advance the cause of Prohibition. It was understood that "Mr. Ayearst assured him that the high Methodist organizations of the land will be solidly behind him in defending his action."[7] In spite of the seriousness of Spracklin's crime, influential forces in Ontario were lining up in his support. Nevertheless, Spracklin's lawyer, R.L. Brackin, anticipated that even after the inquest, manslaughter charges would follow and would be dealt with at the next court sittings or assizes. Early on Monday, Spracklin and McNabb returned to Windsor.

That Monday evening, the Sandwich courtroom was again filled to capacity, and a huge crowd milled about on the streets outside. Everyone was there to hear what Ed Smith, the one man who had been at Babe Trumble's side as he died, had to say. Smith recounted the shooting and insisted that Babe Trumble was not holding a gun as he advanced on Spracklin. Rodd told him that the doctors who were called to attend to Trumble would testify that he was lying and that Smith had told them that Trumble was armed. He denied it. After he was dismissed, Smith turned to Coroner LaBelle and made an unusual request. The coroner nodded his approval, and Smith reached into his pocket and pulled out a small bit of metal and displayed it to the jury. "This is the bullet that killed Trumble" he said in a low voice. "It went thru his body and stung me on the leg. I found it in the lining of my coat." It was a measure of the informality of the proceedings that Spracklin strode forward and examined the bullet. "It is my caliber" he confirmed.[8] To counteract Smith, Rodd called Drs. J. W. Beasley and C. V. Mills who both testified that they had been called to the Chappell House that evening. They both recalled that Smith told them that Trumble came downstairs and that he had pulled out a gun and confronted Spracklin. The final witness was one of the women in the bar that night, a Mrs. Deslippe, who testified that as far as she could recollect, Babe Trumble had no gun.

Everything was now left to the coroner's jury. The very existence of this jury was one of the strangest anomalies in Canadian law. In medieval times, inquests were called by the King to determine the loss of ships, treasure, or the death of a taxpayer, all of which were matters that affected the royal pocketbook. In modern times, the coroner's jury persisted, one of the few administrative juries to continue into the present age. But its role had now become to investigate the circumstances behind a person's death. Its purpose was not to assess guilt or innocence, but rather to ascertain the cause of death.

In order to assist the coroner's jury in making a finding, both Coroner LaBelle and Crown Attorney Rodd gave them instructions. LaBelle made it clear that the entire affair was the result of the nefarious bootlegging business. Skipping over the wisdom of Spracklin and his men breaking into the residence at 3 a.m. without warrants and brandishing guns, LaBelle concluded that Inspector Spracklin "deserved commendation for the campaign he had carried on against the evil which had placed a stigma upon the reputation of the district."

Rodd seconded this commendation. Significantly, he also told the jurors that section 66 of the *OTA* authorized warrantless searches and that Spracklin had every right to break into Trumble's roadhouse that night. In so doing, Rodd may have seriously misled the jurors. Section 66 was indeed a very broad provision which enabled an inspector to enter into any premises to make searches "as he may think necessary." But subsection 66(2) added that a person could refuse entrance to an officer, and the inhabitants of the Chappell House had clearly refused to grant the inspectors permission to enter. The *OTA* went on to provide in section 67 that inspectors could then go to a magistrate and, upon providing "a reasonable ground for belief that any liquor is being kept for sale," a search warrant could be issued. No such warrant had been sought, and in any event, there were no grounds for a warrant.

Traditionally, the Ontario legal system abhorred the notion of warrantless searches. The centuries-old necessity for getting the authority of a magistrate before police could enter a premises shielded citizens from arbitrary police searches. The comment in *Semayne's case* in 1604 that "the house of every one is to him as his castle or fortress" remained fully applicable in 1920. Several judges would later confirm that these protections had not been abrogated by the temperance laws. Nevertheless, Rodd confidently told the jury that Spracklin and his men had a legal right to force open a window and enter the Chappell House at 3 a.m. after having been refused entry. By so instructing the coroner's jury, Rodd may have given them a false sense that Spracklin was just performing his duty. In so doing, there may have been an element of self-protection for it is entirely likely that Rodd had instructed Spracklin that he was within his rights to make warrantless searches. But it would seem that the jurors were never given the possibility of a different point of view; that is, that a group of heavily armed men had, without any authority, broken into a residence in the middle of the night. Under that scenario, they might have concluded that the owner was entitled to take steps to defend his family and property. The shooting of the owner while defending his home might well be considered manslaughter.

Yet J.H. Rodd made certain that no such alternative would be entertained. The jurors were left with the hero inspector, J.O.L. Spracklin, confronting a murder-minded roadhouse operator. The crowd was then cleared from the courtroom while the jury deliberated. Spracklin, his father, and fellow agents waited nervously until the jury returned after an hour. LaBelle read out their verdict in which they found that Beverley

Trumble's death was a justifiable homicide and that his killer, Reverend Leslie Spracklin, had acted in self-defence. Rodd ordered that the crowd that surrounded the courthouse be dispersed so that the Spracklins could leave. The mass of people departed quietly. There was no public demonstration.[9]

Ironically, one of the first mourners for Babe Trumble was Spracklin's mother, Charity. She had retained fond memories of the Trumble family since their Woodstock days and showed a reporter a framed, yellowing photograph of two young men enjoying themselves at the Fort Erie Race Track. They were Beverley Trumble and Willie Spracklin. That Beverley and Willie were pals was not unusual. They were both "sports" of the pre-war period, followers of the race track and prize fighting scene. Charity recalled how "We used to visit the Trumbles of an evening... they sympathized with me when my son was killed."

This grainy 1920 newspaper photo shows the funeral of Babe Trumble.

Lester (right) and Robert Trumble at their father's funeral.

A reporter from the *Detroit News* went to the home of Hamilton Trumble on Giles Boulevard where the casket of Beverley was on view in a darkened room. Lulu appeared to be still in shock as scores of visitors came by to express their condolences. Understandably, she declined to make any comment on the shooting but reminded the reporter that "my children will have to go through life without their father, practically without knowing him."[10] Only hours before the inquest was concluded, Lulu interned her husband. Almost a thousand persons had congregated around Hamilton Trumble's house for the funeral, and many cars, several bearing Michigan plates, were parked nearby. At Windsor Grove Cemetery, Lulu could bear it no more. On the walk up to the mausoleum, she fainted and was held up by a clutch of friends and relatives. Pressing her son Lester to her, she cried out "My God, why did he have to go?"

In the following days, it seemed, at least to Crown Attorney Rodd and local authorities, that the killing of Beverley Trumble was resolved. To them, the finding of self-defence by the coroner's jury was conclusive. However, this verdict was by no means a determination of guilt or innocence, and even Spracklin's own lawyer anticipated that manslaughter charges would be laid.

Justice Rose, who was presiding over the criminal assizes in Sandwich, delayed dismissing the grand jury in anticipation that the charges against Spracklin would be heard. However, as the days went by, no steps were taken and the grand jury was dismissed. On November 11, the Toronto *Globe* declared that the Border Cities had calmed down. It was "now practically assured that no legal action will be taken against him (Spracklin) for the shooting of Beverley Trumble." The unwillingness of the local Crown Attorney to consider criminal charges infuriated the Trumble family, and they demanded that Spracklin be prosecuted by someone other than J.H. Rodd. Forbes Godfrey, the MPP who was so appalled by Spracklin's conduct, stated that "the shooting affair at Windsor is not going to be closed until Spracklin is placed on trial."[11]

While the coroner's jury verdict was a welcome relief to Spracklin's camp, it was apparent that Toronto had to step in if there was going to be a satisfactory resolution. On the Friday, after the jury's decision, Spracklin was given a month's leave "in order to recuperate" from his inspector's job. He would never serve in liquor enforcement again. On November 19, Rodd was called to Attorney General Raney's office in Toronto. Shortly after this closed-door discussion, it was announced that Reverend Spracklin would face a charge of manslaughter at the February 1921 assizes. The following day, he was arraigned and released on bail. More remedial work was obviously necessary. A week later, the "picturesque little band of freelancers" who made up Spracklin's squad were all fired, and Spracklin was replaced by W.J. Lannin, the former Police Chief of Stratford.

Lannin proved to be a breath of fresh air. He was one of the province's most experienced lawmen and currently held the post of District Inspector of Provincial Police. Moreover, he was not prone to making bombastic pronouncements, and instead quietly advised the press that he would be bringing in several veteran officers to patrol the border. Other than that, he declined to discuss any of his plans. Unlike his earnest predecessor, he also showed a puckish sense of humour. He told a group of reporters that he had been thoroughly surprised when he first came to Windsor. The impression he had been given before his arrival was that "a man cannot walk the streets in safety unless he carries a gun." He was impressed at how quiet and respectable it actually appeared.[12]

While the public had been bombarded with editorials praising Spracklin, there was a small but growing undercurrent against the violent and reckless enforcement of temperance laws. Leading the way was the Toronto magazine *Saturday Night.* Consistently skeptical of the prohibition movement, the magazine's editors thought that a great deal of hypocrisy overlay it. For its part, *Saturday Night* was shocked by the "wild west" methods employed by Spracklin and his men, arguing that "in no Canadian city would any police be permitted to go about flourishing weapons and threatening carnage as Spracklin has done since the first day of his appointment." Many police forces did not permit their officers to carry weapons at all. However, Spracklin carried an automatic revolver, the most lethal force available in close quarters. And the fact remained that neither Trumble nor any of the other special agents had fired. Only Spracklin had felt compelled to use his firearm. Before there was a rush to judgment in Spracklin's favour, *Saturday Night* reminded its readers that the evidence of several eyewitnesses in the Chappell House was that Trumble was unarmed. His weapon (if he ever had one) had never been found.

Above all, the editors were saddened that while so many resolutions had been passed by church groups lauding Spracklin, so far not one word of sympathy for the widow or her children had been expressed. They quoted the Reverend T. Albert Moore of the Methodist General Council who pronounced that after having killed his man, the Reverend Spracklin will necessarily "be a more powerful minister in the future." The magazine queried if this was just the first act in a general campaign "of bureaucratic terrorism authorized by the Attorney General of Ontario, and sanctioned by a great and influential religious denomination."

In a subsequent editorial, *Saturday Night* turned its focus on that moral arbiter, the *Christian Guardian*. To the *Guardian*, the tragedy was not that a man lost his life, but that "the law has been shamefully trampled underfoot and counted an unholy thing…and this must be put a stop to." But as *Saturday Night* pointed out the temperance provisions were just provincial regulatory laws, not even crimes as listed in the Criminal Code. Deadly force was being used to seek compliance with a minor regulatory statute. *Saturday Night* was practically the only major publication to call for a halt to the overzealous enforcement of prohibition laws and to warn against the "sanguinary madness (which) seems to have overtaken the more enthusiastic supporters of prohibition (and) which bodes ill for the community."[13] If it was justifiable to kill someone who sold an illegal glass of beer then "it is equally justifiable to kill to induce respect for the snow-cleaning by-laws…" Was it really to be "war to the death on the drinker?"

9

TRIAL: MATTERS OF A "LIMITED COMPASS"

Shortly after he was vindicated at the inquest, Spracklin told a Toronto reporter that "he will continue the fight against the illegal liquor trade with unabated energy." He had no regrets and no apologies to make. Much like the nineteenth-century temperance warriors, Spracklin was convinced that his actions were saving a multitude of others from degradation and death. His was a noble calling. There would never be any question in his mind that the killing of Beverley Trumble was entirely justified.

In the weeks leading up to the trial, the public was given further information on the peculiar operations of the Reverend and his special constables. For one thing, Spracklin's men were targeting specific groups. The raid after Sunday Mass at Assumption Church was a clear signal that his squad distrusted Catholics.

It was true that the Catholic Bishop, Michael Fallon, had publicly indicated his objection to the temperance law as a violation of personal choice. Should Catholics therefore be subject to summary inspections? To Spracklin's specials, the answer was clearly yes. Taking an entire congregation to task was appropriate, and there was nothing untoward in humiliating and searching a large number of Catholics after one of their religious services. As Windsor lawyer A.F. Healy told the provincial committee, such conduct "is engendering in our district a religious or a race cry. There are certain people being intimidated and certain others who are not."[1] Of course, it would have been unthinkable for liquor inspectors to conduct a similar search at the Central Methodist Church.

Nor were Catholics the only group under suspicion. Most of the waiters at the Chappell House were black, a situation attributable to the prejudices of the age when other more lucrative factory work was denied to black workers. Babe Trumble had no trouble in hiring black staff who proved more than loyal to their employer. As the *Toronto Evening Telegram* described one incident, law officers were prevented from inspecting the Chappell House by a man "backed up by several negroes." This only reinforced the perception of the road house operations as belonging to the "others."

Attorney General Raney so much as admitted this in a speech where he noted that some defied the law because they were criminals, but that there were "others who did not have the advantage of birth in a country where law is respected…these, like children, must be educated and taught to respect the law." Liquor inspectors in Windsor would be shocked to discover in places such as the Hungarian Club that women "have the same rights to enjoy the privilege of having beer as the men members" and that in the Polish War Veteran's Association "men and women drinking with babes in arms not over three or four months old." These Eastern Europeans with their casual approach to enjoying beer certainly offended Raney's sensibilities; they would have to be taught.

Catholics, blacks, and Eastern Europeans were not the only minorities to attract the special squad's attention. Jewish rumrunners were often the subject of comment in the *Border Cities Star*, which presumed that the Montreal operators who fed the local bootleggers were Jews who had no regard for Ontario law. In late December, Spracklin's arrest and prosecution of Rabbi Samuel Abramson came before the courts. Spracklin had employed a "spotter" to set up a situation in which Abramson was induced to illegally sell liquor. Spotters, frequently gullible-looking young men, were paid to provoke a person into making an illegal liquor sale. Magistrate Gundy was appalled that the license officers had gone to the extent of coaxing "a person to commit an illegal act in order to bring a charge against him." There seemed to be enough lawlessness about without Spracklin creating situations in order to entrap someone. Abramson was acquitted.[2] That temperance enforcement fell disproportionately on minorities only added to the area's abhorrence of the liquor regulations, and a general determination to defy them.

Yet by far the most embarrassing case Spracklin instigated involved the cream of Anglo society. Spracklin's raid on the yacht owned by Oscar Fleming, the city's former mayor and one of its most prominent businessmen, led to a widely publicized lawsuit for damages. One of Ontario's most senior judges, W.E. Middleton, conducted the trial in Windsor. In his decision rendered on December 28, 1920, he was awestruck by Spracklin's ignorance of legal forms, not to mention his conspicuous absence of common sense. Obtaining a search warrant (which had to be based on reasonable grounds that liquor was being illegally kept for sale) was not a trivial detail, it was a necessity. Spracklin had committed a trespass "in a way that was of necessity most offensive, for it implied an accusation of the most serious character." *Ontario Temperance Act* or not, Canada was still a society based on laws "and for this reason it is of the utmost importance that those charged with the administration of the law should themselves be discreet and, above all, law-abiding." In harsh language to apply to a law officer, Justice Middleton concluded that Spracklin's conduct was "lawless and ill-advised."[3]

Trials such as this kept the Spracklin name in the public eye, and not in a very flattering light. But the focus of all attention was about to centre on the manslaughter trial for the killing of Beverley Trumble. By February, trial preparations were well under way. The Sandwich Courthouse, which had first seen service during the Crimean War and which by 1921 was in an advanced state of shabbiness, was put into readiness for a major trial. Forty subpoenas, a record for Essex County, were issued in anticipation of the number of witnesses required. A special announcement was made that Chief Justice Sir William Mulock would preside. Mulock was not only one of the most senior and respected jurists of his day, many considered him the "Grand Old Man" of Canada. Born in 1843, he had served during the Fenian raids in 1866 and then in Parliament from 1882 to 1905. For nine years, he had been the Postmaster General in Wilfrid Laurier's cabinet. Mulock had little use for temperance and before Prohibition could take hold, he had laid in a huge stock of rye whisky. A young lawyer who went fishing with him recalled that "towards the end it was almost black- about 120 proof. The old man drank it neat- just shaking it into a drop of water."[4] The appointment of a man of Mulock's caliber signalled the high priority the government placed on the case and its determination to conduct a trial beyond reproach.

Mulock's reputation preceded him and on the weekend of his arrival in the Border Cities, the Statler Hotel in Detroit offered Sir William one of their premium rooms. He declined. He was charged with administering His Majesty's laws and staying in a foreign country would be inappropriate. The sheriff arranged

The Sandwich Courthouse where Spracklin's trial was held is pictured here in 1920.

for accommodations at the far more common British-American hotel in Windsor. On Monday, February 21, 1921, the grand jury was convened in the Sandwich Courthouse to consider the manslaughter charge against the Reverend Spracklin. The grand jury's task was not to evaluate the case, but simply to consider if there was enough evidence to warrant a trial. This step was largely a formality, and a true bill authorizing a trial on a charge of manslaughter was issued. While an accusation of murder requires the prosecution to demonstrate deliberation and a pre-existing intent to kill, manslaughter includes unlawful killings that are the result of spontaneous or careless acts. Spracklin himself showed no surprise when he was informed that he would face a jury the next day. He supposed that his bail would be revoked and asked the jail governor how comfortable were the beds in the Sandwich lock-up. He need not have worried. The Crown Attorney was quite content that the minister should remain free during his trial.

Hamilton Trumble had eagerly been following every detail of the case, and was in the courtroom when the grand jury returned the true bill. Elated, he proceeded to the sheriff's office just to make sure "that murderer Spracklin was still there." An offended Spracklin informed associate prosecutor George Urquhart that if Trumble was not removed that "he would not be answerable for the consequences." Urquhart gave orders that the parties were to be kept apart.

By 8 a.m., three hours before the court convened on February 22, the courtroom was packed and officers locked the doors. Those unable to gain admission gathered in excited knots outside on Sandwich Street.

A *Detroit News* reporter noted the "strong sprinkling of ministerial black" in the crowd. The Methodist Church was lining up solidly behind one of their own.[5] The Spracklin family arrived *en masse*, accompanied by O.H. Graham of Walkerville Methodist, and were escorted directly to places at the front of the courtroom. The *News* reporter described the remainder of those who sought places in the chamber. Several were soberly dressed parishioners. Others were flashily dressed women and men with loud overcoats from the bootlegging crowd. The Detroiters were impressed by the proceedings, and the *News* reporter observed that:

> The trappings of the trial were interesting and unfamiliar to the American eye, smacking of the old world. The dapper Crown attorney in gown and starched stock, the sheriff in frock coat, sword and cocked hat, were strange to those who had seen only Detroit's far more informal courts in action.[6]

After the charges had been read and the jury empanelled, the prosecution rose to present its case. In lieu of Rodd, whose presence had been recognized as creating a conflict of interest, the Attorney General's office brought in A. Munro Grier of Niagara to prosecute. A stolid, experienced prosecutor, Grier had the advantage of having no ties to any of the parties. After the charges were read and a jury empanelled, Grier succinctly explained the Crown's case:

> The fact remains that on November 6, Beverley Trumble was a living being, the same as you and I,

141

and on November 7 he was a corpse, and the prisoner
at the bar was responsible for his death. It is your duty
to say whether he was justified in taking the life of a
fellow being.[7]

As for the prisoner at the bar, he sat alone in the dock, a
raised platform in the middle of the courtroom that faced
the judge's bench. A *Detroit Free Press* reporter felt that
Spracklin appeared to be "under great mental stress" and
that "his eyes appeared to be bloodshot." From time to
time he leaned forward to talk to his counsel, R.L. Brackin
of Chatham. Only days after Spracklin had been appointed
an inspector, Brackin had defended a person arrested in
one of his raids. When Spracklin took the stand, Brackin
subjected him to a relentless cross-examination. Perhaps
impressed by his skill as a defence counsel, Spracklin had
decided to use Brackin's talents for his own benefit.

It was not until the afternoon that the first witness,
Dr. W.C. Pepin, was called to the stand. Pepin had

The lawyers for the Spracklin trial are pictured here, flanking Chief
Justice Sir William Mulock. At left is A. Munro Grier, special Crown
Prosecutor, and at right is R.L. Brackin, Spracklin's chief counsel.

conducted the post-mortem and discovered two bullet wounds, one in the lower left abdomen and the other in the right leg. The abdominal wound had severed the femoral artery and Trumble had bled to death. Pepin's findings might have been expected to arouse some surprise, for at the inquest all the evidence had suggested that Spracklin had only fired once. The doctor indicated that Spracklin had fired twice when

Lulu Trumble and her son.

no one else had fired at all. It was an intriguing fact which was not followed up, and which was all but overlooked in the sensation created by the following witness.

Lulu Bell Trumble, Babe's widow, took the stand next. Conscious that this was her public moment, she was again dressed in a striking black gown. Moreover, she appeared with the deceased's children, Lester and Robert. Aware of the emotional impact of having the victim's children gazing at the jury while the widow/mother testified, Mulock ordered that the children be removed. They went to sit with their grandfather Hamilton, who had positioned himself immediately behind the prisoner's box. Lulu related the story of the shooting much as she had described it at the inquest. She was not feeling well and had gone to bed. Then she heard some shouting downstairs and someone called out Spracklin's name. Tiptoeing downstairs, she saw Spracklin and the two

Bell brothers with their weapons drawn. As for Babe, he had been getting her a hot water bottle, which he had laid aside. Carrying nothing but a cigarette, he had gone down the stairs. She heard him call out and demand to see Spracklin's search warrant. Then she heard the shot and saw her husband collapse into Ed Smith's arms. At the moment of the shooting she was sure that Babe was unarmed.

Under cross-examination, she conceded that Babe had once been convicted of an *OTA* offence that disqualified him from running a roadhouse. As a result, he had passed on the operation of the Chappell House to his partner, Aylmer Orton, and no longer was involved in the day-to-day running of the roadhouse. No doubt this was a convenient arrangement, except that Trumble still owned and lived on the premises and gave orders to the staff. Orton was a Detroiter who was unable to cross the border. She admitted that thanks to the publicity from Spracklin's accusations they had lost a large part of their American clientele. To Brackin's suggestions that her husband always carried a gun and that he had been armed that night, Lulu gave a firm and consistent denial. Shotguns were the only weapons she claimed to have seen in the Chappell House. She recounted how the day after the shooting, Constable Snider of the Sandwich police made an attempt at following police procedures and had conducted a perfunctory search of the Chappell House in search of a gun. He found nothing.

Lulu was followed by Ed Smith, who gave a graphic description of Spracklin gunning down a defenseless man. The prosecutor asked:

Q: ...first, was there any doubt Trumble had a pistol in his hand that evening?

A: He had not a pistol.

Q: Then I asked you if the only pistols you saw were the pistols you had seen in the hands of the officers?

A: Yes.

His Lordship (Mulock): Did you see a pistol in Trumble's hand?

A: No.

Q: How do you know?

A: I was standing right beside him.[8]

Smith was standing so close that, after penetrating Trumble, the bullet had also struck his leg and left a substantial bruise.

When his opportunity came, Brackin established that Smith, a native of Winnipeg but an itinerant soul, was an unsavoury fellow, a follower of the race track circuit, and a professional bettor. Having established in the eyes of the jury that Smith was a less than model citizen, Brackin confronted him with the statements of two doctors who said that Smith had told them that Trumble had a gun. He denied ever making such a statement. The prosecutor also pointed out that inspector Frank Bell would swear that immediately after the shooting, he asked Smith for Trumble's gun. Smith replied, "Don't bother about that now. Bev will come to in a minute and be delirious. Don't bother for a minute or two." Smith denied the conversation. Brackin then took Smith through his bizarre conduct after the shooting. He had immediately left Sandwich and caught the ferry to Detroit where he had registered at a hotel under (as Smith phrased it) a "consumed" name. The purpose of getting out of the jurisdiction, Brackin suggested, was to get rid of Trumble's gun. This was also denied.

The following day, Wednesday, February 23, the Crown's case became seriously undone. Ernest Deslippe, the man found on the ground outside the Chappell House, died overnight of pneumonia in Hôtel Dieu Hospital. Other than his previous statement which was read to the jury, whatever he had to contribute to the case was forever lost. Grier then called Jack Bannon, another one of Trumble's entourage. It might not have been expected at the time, but Bannon's testimony would become the trial's pivotal turning points. At first, his testimony was consistent with Smith's, and he confirmed that he had never seen Trumble with a gun. Prosecutor Grier pressed him on this point:

Q: You told me you did not see Trumble with a gun?

A: I didn't see Trumble with a gun.

Q: Either before or after the shooting?

A: No. sir.

Brackin had undoubtedly taken the opportunity to question all of the Crown witnesses prior to the trial. He knew what he wanted to get from Bannon, and was ready to pounce. For his part, Bannon nervously fingered a gold crucifix, and waited for Brackin's first question:

Q: After you went into the doorway leading from the little hallway into the private dining room, you saw Trumble, and Trumble said "I am shot." You saw Mrs. Trumble. Did Mrs. Trumble have a gun in her hands?

A: Yes.

It was a startling revelation, a concession from a prosecution witness that Trumble had access to a weapon. Realizing the significance of this disclosure, a number of persons in the courtroom broke into applause. An outraged Mulock demanded that the demonstration cease and that the culprits stand up "if they were men" so they could be cited for contempt. Not surprisingly, no one stood.

The defence had scored a major coup by confirming through the mouth of one of Trumble's gang that Lulu was lying and that a gun was present. And yet, Bannon, a witness that the defence would all but adopt, never said that he had seen Trumble threatening anyone with a revolver, only that Lulu had been armed. Nevertheless, the defence was now able to suggest that Babe Trumble may have had access to a weapon, that Lulu may have given it to him, or that she had seized it after the shooting.

Later that morning, Brackin began the case for the defence. He started by painting a picture of Beverley

Trumble as a violent man with an abiding hatred of Leslie Spracklin. A tailor recounted how one day he had noticed Trumble casually remove a revolver from his pocket as he was changing clothes. A mechanic testified that he had repaired a 38 caliber Smith & Wesson at Trumble's request. Carrying a revolver was an occupational requirement in the bootlegging profession, and it should not have come as a surprise that Babe Trumble was armed. More importantly, these neutral witnesses effectively confirmed that Lulu was lying and that Trumble regularly carried a handgun. Evelyn Bell, Spracklin's sister, described how she had once gone to Bob-Lo Island recreation park with her children and encountered Trumble. He told her to tell her brother to get out of the license inspector business for, "He will be shot if he doesn't get off the job. They will shoot a man quicker for whisky than they will for money. He wants to get off the job before he is killed." She relayed this to her brother, who perceived it as a threat. However, it was equally plausible that Trumble was not threatening anyone, and if anything, he was conveying a warning that others meant to harm Spracklin.

Having laid out a sketch of the participants, Brackin moved on to the early morning of November 6. Mark Heaton repeated the testimony he'd given at the inquest. He had been in the bar when he heard Trumble shouting at the Bell brothers to show their badges. Heaton went through the hallway and into the living room, where he saw the confrontation and instantly seized Trumble's gun with his left hand and moved to strike him with his right. However, Ed Smith pinned him down from behind and dragged him from the room. After the shooting, Heaton had reentered the living room and made a further observation he had omitted at the inquest. Some of Trumble's clothing had been removed to expose his wound, and it was apparent that he was wearing a pistol holster and that a gun lay on the floor.

The Bell brothers confirmed that they had been confronted by an armed Trumble and had retreated from the dining room. Frank Bell stated that Trumble's gun had been touching him when he heard Spracklin give the "back squad" order. The Bells left the living room, and the only two men present when the shot was fired were Trumble and Spracklin. He heard only one shot. Frank Bell asked Smith for Trumble's revolver, but the later declined and explained that when Trumble regained consciousness he would demand it back.

All of this was the preliminary to Spracklin himself entering the witness box. As an accused, he was not required to testify, but in light of the allegations he no doubt felt that he had to clear his name. According to the *Border Cities Star,* "His appearance in the box stilled the subdued murmurs and hums of the court room, and during the succeeding two hours, breathless silence reigned."[9] The defence began by taking him through the night of June 1920 in which he had stood outside the Chappell House watching the drunks come and go. Spracklin had barely begun to recount those events than Mulock ruled that it was all irrelevant to the manslaughter charge and ordered Brackin to move on. More pertinent was Spracklin's recollection of the times when he had encountered a threatening Babe Trumble. Late the previous September, the two men clashed outside the Dominion House tavern in Sandwich. While he had done nothing to arouse suspicion, Spracklin insisted on going through Trumble's car. "I'll be damned if you can search my car without a warrant," Trumble shouted in reply. Spracklin refused to back down, and the situation was finally defused when Lulu opened the back trunk. Spracklin examined it and found nothing. The two men parted with Trumble calling Spracklin "nothing but a dirty, low-down cur, and you'll get yours."

Spracklin confirmed that during the preceding Friday evening he had driven past the Chappell House several times, but nothing had aroused his suspicions. After being called out early that morning and discovering Ernie Deslippe on the lawn, he had decided to enter the premises. When his men failed to force the front door, they tried one of the windows and used this to gain entrance. In the bar area he encountered a number of men including Bill Morton, Jack Bannon, and Ed Smith. They discussed Deslippe's beating for a few moments until Spracklin decided to use this opportunity to see if any illegal liquor was in storage. As Spracklin rummaged through the bar, he heard Trumble loudly demanding that the intruders show their badges or get out. He ran towards the tumult through the pantry and entered the kitchen. He took up a position by the door where he saw Trumble in the private dining room pointing a gun at the Bell brothers:

> I drew my gun from its holster, and covered Trumble, who was still backing the Bell boys toward the door. He had backed them toward the door when I called out, "Back squad, we don't want any trouble like this."
>
> Trumble was in the doorway when I called. He swung his gun around and saw me, and said "_____

you, Spracklin. I'll shoot you." His gun was three or four inches from my stomach, at least a .38 calibre Colt.

As Spracklin recounted the incident, a reporter felt that "he broke down at the moment he told of firing the fatal shot (and) sighs of sympathy swept across the crowded court room." He continued:

> I looked into his (Trumble's) eyes, and what I saw there made me believe that he intended to do as he said. I dropped my gun down to my hip—and—
>
> Mr. Spracklin was unable to continue his evidence at this point. Manifestly laboring under painful emotion, with tears filling his eyes, he dropped his head and remained standing in the witness stand for several surcharged seconds.
>
> "You fired?" inquired Mr. Brackin.
>
> "Yes" was the almost inaudible reply.

Spracklin insisted that they were alone at the time of the shooting. Furthermore, he was afraid that as Trumble's men were armed (although none of them had produced any weapons), to avoid an all-out gun battle it was prudent for the inspectors to leave. Spracklin exited through the same window used to gain entrance. He crossed Sandwich Street and remained hidden behind a small building until he saw doctors and the Sandwich police arrive at the Chappell House. Getting into a car driven by Mark Heaton, he instructed him to drive to the Windsor Police Station. "I had been continually opposed in Sandwich and I felt I was not safe in the hands of Sandwich police."

Brackin attempted to sum up by asking Spracklin's state of mind in those few crucial seconds:

> "What was your belief in the moment before you fired?" questioned Brackin.
> "I believed thoroughly that he was going to carry out his threat." Mr. Spracklin replied.

For his part, Crown Attorney Grier was lacking in sympathy. He questioned Spracklin why he and his men turned and fled instead of offering assistance to the man he had just shot. Spracklin simply responded, "I withdrew from the place." He further admitted to Grier that he had no training in police work and that his only knowledge of his duties came from reading the *Ontario Temperance Act*. There were many things about policing that Spracklin was even now just finding out about. His weapon, an automatic pistol, was not standard police issue. Neither did he have a permit authorizing him to carry it. Despite his comments about Trumble as a malevolent presence, at no time during his three months as a liquor inspector had Spracklin actually searched the Chappell House. This was singularly curious as Spracklin's prominence had arisen out of his attacks on the Sandwich police for failing to raid that house of infamy. But when he was in charge, Spracklin had also chosen to give it a wide passage. He gave two reasons. First, his wife asked him every morning not to go there. Second, he had the satisfaction if knowing that "the Chappell House business was, to the best of my knowledge, largely at a standstill" and no further measures were needed. How he would know that without investigating is difficult to understand.

Spracklin did admit to Grier that the cumulative effect of the warnings he had received, the gunfights he had been in, as well as the shots that had been fired at his home, had left him in a highly agitated frame of mind. When he encountered Babe Trumble in the kitchen waving a gun and demanding to see badges, he was (in Grier's words) in a "condition of fear." On that note, Grier ended his cross-examination and announced that Lulu would be recalled to the stand. A buzz of excitement shot through the courtroom crowd as the widow again took the witness box. She refuted everything that had been said by the defence witnesses, and in response to Bannon's assertion that she had a pistol, she said, "If I had a gun there would certainly have been another murder." Lulu Trumble was a formidable figure, and no one questioned that assertion.

It was now late in the evening on the second day of the trial, and all of the evidence had been presented. Fifty years later, a manslaughter trial would likely consume several days if not weeks, and be interrupted by several lengthy procedural objections. However, in 1921 only the facts mattered, and both counsel had expeditiously placed the case before the jury.

The following morning, it was up to the lawyers. As his client had already testified, the defence counsel, Brackin, was the first to address the jury. He wasted no time in appealing to their emotions and informing them that this case had its roots in the hatred that Beverley Trumble held for the Reverend Spracklin. This hatred manifested itself in threats, insults, and ultimately in confronting him with a pistol. Citing scripture, Brackin compared Spracklin to Jesus Christ driving the money lenders from the temple. Our Lord had not waited for properly endorsed search warrants, and neither had Spracklin. All of the defence evidence and even some of the Crown's suggested that Trumble was armed and threatening murder. As for the defence witnesses, he dismissed Ed Smith as a man who "had thug written all over him." In the case of Lulu Trumble, "she lied and she lied and she lied." In order to believe her it would be necessary to disbelieve almost every other witness who had come before the Court. He then held up the accused Leslie Spracklin as a "he-man" doing what a hero should do to protect his community. A real man would protect his neighbourhood from foul conduct for "the real man would hate to see his sister or his mother smoking cigarettes and drinking whisky." Such abominations had to be stopped, by armed force if necessary.

For the prosecution, Munro Grier had little to work with. He began by suggesting that the tragedy was entirely of Spracklin's making. It was he who had forced his way into the Chappell House at 3 a.m. without any justification. While the rest of his men were backing out, it was Spracklin who stood his ground, escalating the situation. Even these comments were undercut when Justice Mulock instructed the jury that Spracklin was within his rights as an inspector to have broken into the Chappell House and was lawfully there right up until the moment of the shooting. In so doing, Mulock tipped the scales in Spracklin's favour by exonerating him from creating a dangerous and illegal situation which had led to a man losing his life. As for the facts, Mulock instructed the jury that they were of "limited compass." The only relevant matters were those few urgent seconds that preceded Spracklin's gun shot. It was up to the jurors to consider the state of Spracklin's mind. If he could have avoided killing, it was his duty to do so. If killing was his only way to save his own life, then he was innocent. This was not a question of whether the jurors supported or opposed the *OTA,* nor of Spracklin's status as a clergyman or as an enforcement officer, for "If a man offends he must be punished. If he does not offend, he must be acquitted." After the judge's address the jury retired to consider their verdict, and the courtroom was cleared of everyone but Spracklin, his men, and his family.

The result could not seriously have been in doubt. There was substantial evidence from the defence and even from one Crown witness that Trumble was armed or had access to arms. There was also a strong reason to believe that Spracklin's life was being threatened. A charge of manslaughter had to be proven beyond a reasonable doubt and the evidence fell well short of that standard. The jury deliberated for scarcely an hour before they returned to the courtroom and gave a verdict of acquittal. Spracklin left the prisoner's dock and was embraced by his family. His mother, Charity, insisted on thanking each member of the jury for her son's deliverance. No member of the Trumble family was present. Sir William Mulock again repeated dire warnings in the event of any public demonstrations, but his energies were wasted. The Sandwich crowd shrugged

A banner headline in the *Border Cities Star* announces Spracklin's acquittal, 1921.

and hastily departed. The reaction of Protestant Ontario would not be so subdued.

When news of the acquittal was relayed to the Ontario legislature, a congratulatory clapping on desks broke out among United Farmers members. The Opposition and cabinet members kept a discreet silence. At a prohibition rally at Massey Hall, the participants were in the middle of a hymn when news of the acquittal was suddenly announced. The hymn of praise was abruptly cut short as the crowd shouted out "three cheers and a tiger" for their champion. The *Toronto Evening Telegram* found that "thousands of otherwise normal people regard Mr. Spracklin's acquittal as a triumph for their views." This verdict was just, concluded the *Toronto Daily Star*, for "Mr. Spracklin was menaced by the victim of the tragedy when he fired the shot... At the time of the shooting he was acting as the agent of the community securing respect for its laws." It was all so sordid, and the *Daily Star* prayed that "the Trumble tragedy, the rum-running along the frontier that has humiliated this country and corrupted whole communities" could be brought to an end. The only possible solution was total Prohibition and an affirmative vote on the upcoming April referendum to stop all liquor imports into Ontario from Quebec. Only then would Ontario be able to "lift up its head."[10]

On the Sunday after his acquittal, Spracklin was received in Sarnia by no less a figure than the Reverend Samuel Chown, the General Superintendant of the Methodist Church. A crowd estimated at over 2,000 listened while Dr. Chown compared Spracklin to Korean protesters who had defied their Japanese oppressors. "If it is wrong to denounce wrong, then Reverend J.O.L. Spracklin was wrong in denouncing the insidious things he saw with his own eyes." To Chown, Spracklin was the gallant leader who had "figuratively raised the fiery cross of Methodism against the liquor forces in preparation for the referendum on April 18."

Yet, in the months leading up to that referendum, the people of the border took a different lesson from the Chappell House shooting.

10

LEARNING TO LIVE
WITH BOOZE

I t is difficult to gauge popular reaction to the verdict. There were no polls conducted to measure the level of support or infamy that Spracklin attracted. Perhaps one way of testing the reaction of border residents was their approach to the upcoming referendum on the proposal to ban all alcohol imports into Ontario. Barely a month after the acquittal verdict, a reporter from the Toronto *Globe* who was covering the referendum canvassed the border area and was shocked to discover just how hostile residents were to Prohibition. "In Windsor bootlegging apparently has been raised to the dignity of a profession" he discovered, "and it is probably the only city in Ontario where it may claim to figure as one of the basic industries."[1]

Only a week before the scheduled vote to ban alcohol imports, an event was held at the Windsor Armouries that seemed to epitomize local attitudes towards the forces of moral uplift. The Armouries had been rented by the Dominion Alliance for a huge rally in support of the Prohibition cause. A band was hired and a ladies choir offered hymns while their banner, bearing the admonition "'Dry' clean the Border Cities," was carried to the front of the speaker's platform. But it was apparent that many if not most of the 4,000 individuals who crammed into the Armouries were "wets" who intended to disrupt the meeting. Both forces waited on the evening's speaker, William E. "Pussyfoot" Johnson, to begin his address. As a special agent for the Department of the Interior, he earned his nickname by his cat-like stealth in creeping up on and raiding saloons. By the end of his career, he had secured over 4,400 convictions in raids on blind pigs, gambling spots, and bordellos. From there he had gone on to become one of America's foremost temperance advocates. Nothing deterred him, for on a speaking tour in England he had been viciously assaulted and lost an eye. Prohibitionists in Ontario had enlisted Johnson to make a swing through the province in support of the cause. However, the majority of the Windsor crowd, particularly the men in the Armouries gallery, seemed to be in no mood to listen to a temperance sermon. Many of them were returned veterans and in lieu of hymns they were belting out "I Want To Go Home" and its refrain:

Take me over the sea where the snipers they can't get at me
Oh my, I don't want to die, I want to go home.

The men kept up a steady cacophony of song and noise and refused to let any of the clergymen be heard. Windsor's Police Chief Daniel Thompson mounted the

Pussyfoot Johnson barely escaped with his life after a rally-turned-riot in Windsor on April 11, 1921.

stage and pleaded with the crowd to at least listen to a Windsor preacher. They refused.

Nevertheless, the ever-smiling Johnson entered the hall to a faint chorus of applause and a barrage of hisses. He seemed to take in the hubbub good-naturedly and beamed to his few supporters in the audience. Unable to be heard, he unfurled a large version of the referendum ballot with the "X" marked over the "yes" for the ban on imports. A *Globe* reporter who was present felt that "the audience at once resolved itself into a maelstrom of contending factions." Windsor's entire police force was present, but unable to deal with such a headstrong mob. In the midst of the uproar, Dr. Oaten from the Dominion Alliance called out "British fair play" and "There are ladies present, are you gentlemen or hoodlums?" After several more minutes of chaos he concluded, "You are hoodlums."[2] Unable to make himself heard, Johnson picked up a glass of water and took a long, dramatic swallow. This display of healthy water-drinking was the last straw for the outraged crowd, and they prepared to rush the stage. Chief Thompson realized that the situation was rapidly deteriorating and that the angry throng meant to do Johnson severe physical harm. Aided by a few other officers, Thompson grabbed Johnson and squeezed him out one of the Armouries side doors. Johnson and his police escort ran down Ouellette Avenue in a direct line toward the Detroit ferry. At their heels was a mob that had lost none of its enthusiasm for ripping Johnson limb from limb. Once they arrived at the ferry dock, the police immediately shoved Johnson onto a boat and barely succeeded in holding off the crowd until the gangplank was raised and the vessel was safely on its way to Detroit.

That a significant number of Border Cities residents were prepared to lynch a Prohibition advocate revealed the depth of public feelings against the humiliations caused from the enforcement of the temperance laws. The searches, the questions, and the daily irritants thrust on them by inspectors from Toronto seemed to be reaching a breaking point.

The April referendum again confirmed the area's stubborn opposition to temperance. In Ford City, fewer that ten percent of voters wanted the importation of liquor stopped. Sandwich voted 650 to 161 to keep up the imports. The results proved that northern Essex County was irredeemably "wet" and a substantial majority wanted the free flow of liquor to continue. In Toronto, Prohibition crowds followed the provincial results at a public meeting where "Windsor's wet total received laughter and various humorous remarks." However, the last laugh was on the prohibitionists, for Toronto also voted to keep the imports. While the margin was tighter than in Windsor, big cities such as Toronto and Hamilton had also had enough of

The results of the 1921 referendum.

Prohibition and wanted to restore easy access to alcohol. Not so rural Ontario. In the final tally, 540,773 voted in favour of forbidding imports and only 373,938 against.

Attorney General Raney thought that this result entrenched the era of Prohibition, and that solid enforcement of the temperance laws would inevitably follow. He would never concede that employing a fanatic such as Spracklin was a mistake, for he believed that the principle of Prohibition was sound. The program only required diligent execution. In an essay that was published in the *Border Cities Star*, Raney hammered the point that temperance was the law of Ontario and must be obeyed. Anyone who defied the liquor laws (which included a large proportion of the Border Cities population) "proclaims himself to be both an outlaw and a traitor." Using Great War rhetoric, he challenged the liquor interests: "The fight is on, and they are releasing their poisonous gas in great clouds... the assault is not only upon the prohibitory laws, but upon the reign of law."[3]

Whether the Border Cities agreed with this call to arms was irrelevant, for they were about to be dragged into Raney's sober new Ontario whether they wanted to be or not. On July 18, 1921, the import ban came into effect, and Windsor warehouses that had previously held huge stocks of liquor were emptied. In the preceding days, long queues formed outside the British American and Walkerville breweries to cart off cases of nine-percent beer. Legally, the Border Cities became dry. The reality was quite different, as suppliers found new sources and the attempt to limit stocks only made those that were available all the more valuable.

After the July 1921 rules came into effect, a Toronto reporter asked one Windsor bootlegger how he could stay in business with these added restrictions. "A far-away look came into his eyes," the reporter noted, "and he repeated that 'he would get it.' But how remained a secret." Small-scale distilleries blossomed across Essex County as country folk tried their hand at manufacturing alcohol. As the Detroit *Free Press* reported, one way to get liquor was to steal it from those who had it. One crew of "liquor pirates" docked at the mouth of Little River in Riverside just east of Windsor and preyed on other rum runners who were in mid-river. Armed gangs combed the downriver area in search of liquor caches and the crackle of gun fire became a nightly occurrence along the Detroit River. The *Free Press* reported that "Citizens in the west end of Windsor are in a state of semi-panic at the failure of the police department to check the bold operations of the daring gang of thieves."[4] Lawlessness had reached the point where the residents were discussing forming armed civilian patrols to protect themselves.

Six months after the end of the Spracklin trial, when the forces of goodness had supposedly prevailed, a decision in a Windsor court effectively upended everything the authorities had considered to be the proper application of the law. In the summer of 1921, Sandwich police seized a shipment of beer from the British American Brewery that had cleared the export dock and was awaiting shipment to Wyandotte, Michigan. The brewers sued to have their property returned to them, and hired some of the most knowledgeable constitutional lawyers to press their case. The issue came before Windsor's Magistrate W.E. Gundy on August 10, 1921. He ruled that breweries such as the British American had been licensed by the federal government in Ottawa to produce their product. These breweries were further at liberty to ship those products to the United States or any other foreign country. This was a matter of international trade and there was nothing in the provincial temperance laws (nor could there be) which interfered with that trade. Gundy noted for the record that in just the last few months, "Rev. J.O.L. Spracklin was in charge of license department work here, cases of a similar nature were frequently brought to court by him, prosecuting bootleggers caught in the act of smuggling liquor to the United States." The lawyer for the breweries conceded that "That may be the case" and added that what Inspector Spracklin was doing was obviously illegal. "As for Mr. Spracklin," the lawyer continued, "I would be perfectly satisfied to have him lead me into the Kingdom of Heaven, but as far as the law is concerned I would not place much faith in the prosecutions he has made."[5]

The magistrate agreed, and the authorities were ordered to return the beer shipment to the British American Brewing Company. Gundy's decision was a bombshell and was widely reported across North America. The day after the ruling, the *New York Herald* noted, "Magistrate Gundy expressed the opinion that the United States was big enough to take care of its own laws." Within hours, the significance of his decision began to sink in. Rum running was not illegal, and there was no impediment (on the Canadian side) to exporting alcohol to the United States. Spracklin's speed boat pursuing and blazing away at rum runners bound for the U.S. shore had all been contrary to the law. The day after Gundy's ruling, huge shipments of alcohol began to leave the export docks of the Border Cities bound for Michigan shores. Train loads of beer marked as "hay" with a few loads of real horse fodder by the doors were leaving Windsor on an hourly basis. Customs laws only permitted clearance papers to be issued during daylight hours, but beer-heavy freighters left at sundown and tarried by the downriver shoals until it was safe to evade American lawmen. As the *Border Cities Star* recorded, "In the last 48 hours since Judge Gundy handed down his decision virtually declaring the export of beer from Ontario to the United States legal, large amounts of beer have been taken over to the Michigan shore..." While a Hiram Walker spokesman primly announced that even with this ruling the distillery would not sell whisky in the United States "as a matter of principle," (they would do so through third parties) Windsor breweries began working at full capacity to supply their American customers. A total of seventy-five Michigan state troopers were called out to patrol the forty mile long Detroit River in a futile attempt to stem the flow.[6]

By December 1921, statistics for the sale of beer to the Detroit area from the Canada were astronomical. More than 1,000 cases were being shipped daily and barges filled with nine-percent beer were sailing across the river nightly. James R. Davis, Michigan's director of prohibition, was astounded when confronted with the statistics from the Canadian export docks. Obviously, a few troopers were having little impact on stopping these imports. As for Detroit itself, by the middle of 1923, most reasonable observers concluded that Prohibition had been a resounding failure. The *Detroit News* reported that over 3,000 blind pigs had replaced the 1,534 licensed saloons that had operated before Prohibition. Shortly after, the newspaper conceded that this was a wild miscalculation and that the city had at least 10,000 spots where liquor could be bought and consumed. "There are blocks and blocks in certain sections of the city in which every house is either a bootleg stand or a blind pig." The establishments were all unregulated, open at all hours, and sold products that were often dangerous. Because the bars operated outside the law, bootlegger gangs shot it out on the city streets to control neighbourhoods and supplies for these blind pigs. When asked if Prohibition was being enforced in Michigan, James Davis thought that it was, but he conceded "Not in Detroit."[7] As the 1920s wore on, Detroit would make a separate peace with Prohibition and the police tolerated saloons so long as they governed themselves and did not admit minors. Conducting a personal tour

A Detroit blind pig is raided, 1920s.

of the blind pigs, Mayor John C. Lodge noted that "The crowds were large but not disorderly." While those that were disorderly could expect to be raided, "but for those observing the common rules of propriety, it was business as usual during Lodge's administration."

Much as happened in Detroit, the reality in Ontario was that the major cities such as Toronto, Hamilton, and Windsor had no use for Prohibition. But reconciling the law with reality was never Attorney General Raney's strong point. If anything, Raney and Premier Drury seemed determined to extend the provisions of the *OTA*. While the embarrassment of the Spracklin affair might have served as a lesson to the government that they should tread lightly with regard to forcing morality on the public, Raney was fixed on moving in the opposite direction. Amendments to bolster the *OTA* became regular features of each legislative session. Doctors could arbitrarily have their right to prescribe liquor removed and jail sentences were imposed for second convictions for intoxication. These heavy-handed provisions fed the public perception of the Drury government as a gang of fanatical puritans. To Conservative leader Howard Ferguson, Raney had become "a bully of the law." The *Ottawa Journal* wondered, "Who constituted Mr. Raney the moral arbiter, the conscience of the Province of Ontario…?"[8]

Ultimately the public passed judgment on the United Farmers in the provincial election of May 1923. The attorney general became the lightning rod for the Drury administration. At a Raney rally in Elora, a heckler called out, "Who employed Spracklin?" The flustered attorney general "crashed his fist down on the table. 'Don't let us waste time with this nonsense,' he exclaimed, 'This law is being enforced.'" Surprisingly, the Spracklin affair played little part in the election contest at the border. A.F. Healy, the lawyer who had spoken out against Spracklin before the provincial committee, was running in the North Essex riding. His views had not changed, and he termed the *OTA* "a marked failure, and had even been responsible for horrible results." But while Liberal and Conservative candidates condemned Raney and his bulldog approach towards liquor enforcement, none chose to address the Spracklin affair head-on. Perhaps the unseemly event of a clergyman killing a bootlegger was so distasteful that most simply wanted to ignore it. It was rarely referred to in the campaign. Only newspapers hostile to the United Farmers, such as the Toronto *Evening Telegram,* fixed on misadventures such as the shooting of Babe Trumble as proof of the government's fanaticism. The *Telegram* commented, with questionable geography but firm conviction as to who was responsible, that "It was Raneyism that shot Beverley Trumble. It was Raneyism which went buccaneering on the Windsor river."[9]

The result of the provincial election of 1923 not only brought the defeat of the United Farmers, but also a rejection of moral uplift. Frank Wilson, a Conservative and the lawyer who had consistently headed up the anti-temperance forces, was elected in Windsor. The Conservatives under Howard Ferguson formed a new government, and would move cautiously to re-introduce alcohol back into the legal mainstream of Ontario society. In May 1925, a buzz of excitement went through the Border Cities as workers prepared new "beverage rooms" where real 4.4% beer could legally be served.

At the British American Hotel, "all day long crowds continued to jam the dining room and lobby, where special tables had been set out."[10] In 1927, the *Ontario Temperance Act* was repealed by Ferguson's government and replaced by the *Liquor Control Act*, which enabled the public to buy alcohol. Beginning on June 1, 1927, Windsor residents could go to a government outlet, furtively hand the clerk their request through a secure wicket, and depart with liquor hidden in a brown paper bag. The sin of drinking must remain clandestine, but at least it was now legal.

While the 1920s roared on, the easy availability of alcohol in the Border Cities enabled it to act as a major supplier to the United States. Fortunes were made at the export docks as shipments of whisky and beer made the short run across the Detroit River. James Cooper, for one, used his connections with Hiram Walkers & Sons Distillery to load freighters with premium whisky. One of his colleagues, Harry

A line of inebriated men wait in line at a government outlet to purchase liquor in the 1928 cartoon.

Low, even used a former naval minesweeper, the *Vedas,* to haul thousands of cases of liquor to the United States. Such cargoes were listed as destined for Cuba or the Bahamas, but the ships would arrive back at the Windsor export docks after only a few hours sailing. No one doubted that they had gone farther than a convenient stop along the American shore. The 1927 Royal Commission on Customs and Excise found that bootleggers effectively ran the docks and possessed their own seals which enabled them to label whisky cargoes as "milk" or "canned goods."[11] Mabel Walker Willebrandt, the Assistant Attorney General of the U.S., considered the Detroit River to be one of the main gateways for the illegal liquor trade. As one writer noted, "the Detroit-Windsor borderland (became) the most important point of entry."[12] It was estimated that up to seventy-five percent of all illegal alcohol entering the United States came from the Detroit River area. Spracklin's brief crusade had accomplished nothing beyond costing one man his life and reminding people of the price of fanaticism.

11

THE PARTING GLASS

As for Spracklin's "Flying Squad," that jaunty group of lawmen who had fought to bring temperance to the border, some of them soon resorted to form. In January 1921, Stanley Hallam also shot and killed a person. During a fight with his brother William in a Toronto rooming house, Stanley grabbed a gun, presumably intending to shoot his brother, and instead fired a shot which struck a woman in an adjacent room. At his trial on a charge of manslaughter that March, Hallam was surprisingly enough acquitted. In June 1921, barely half a year after they had been discharged as liquor inspectors, both Stanley and William Hallam were found guilty of assault and robbery. Replicating the techniques they had brought to perfection in Essex County, the Hallams had purchased a liquor shipment in Kent County. When the time came for payment, they pulled out their guns, announced that they were police officers, and declared that the liquor was confiscated. This time they did not get away with it, and a conviction was registered against them. As the 1920s wore on, Stanley Hallam was also convicted of car theft, served a year in Burwash Reformatory, and upon his release, broke his parole and fled to the United States.[1] It is amazing in retrospect to consider that Spracklin selected a person such as Stanley Hallam, a career criminal, as a law officer to assist him in enforcing the temperance laws.

At least Babe Trumble's entourage was a proper group of villains, and predictably enough they continued in their chosen profession. Jack Bannon, the witness who had fingered his gold cross while on the stand, and whose testimony had done so much to vindicate Spracklin, had not turned over a new leaf. Throughout the 1920s, he continued to ship and sell illegal liquor and occasionally worked the other side of the fence by acting as a police informer. In 1934, he played a major role in the widely reported kidnapping of beer tycoon John Labatt. At Bannon's trial in October 1935, he gave his occupation as real estate, but when pressed on the point admitted that he was "a railway man and was later in the whisky and beer business." He was convicted and sentenced to fifteen years in prison.

As for any embarrassment caused by Spracklin's specials, this was all but forgotten in the euphoria following his vindication. The embodiment of a muscular, assertive Christianity, he was rapturously embraced by Protestant Ontario. A few days after his acquittal, Spracklin appeared in London and played a hockey game after a church service. Spectators crowded into the arena to get a look at the famous clergyman, and he was given a standing ovation. At the Park Street Methodist

Church in Chatham, 1200 people jammed the church to listen to their champion. From there, his triumphal tour proceeded to Paris, Ontario, where he preached a thunderous temperance sermon. His was not the easy route, he cautioned his listeners, for there were many evil-intentioned men who wished him harm. There was a pro-liquor "Determination League" in Toronto who were sending him death threats and promising to shoot him down if he ever dared enter their city. He bravely announced that he would pay no attention to this threat and that he would proceed to Toronto whenever the occasion arose. While Spracklin often proclaimed that he was the focus of hate from the liquor interests, there is no record of any one seriously threatening him.

Moreover, there was always an element of self-pity about these pronouncements, of what Spracklin had suffered for the cause. He reminded the Paris congregation that "I had to go through the tragedy of killing a man."[2] In this, he displayed a peculiar lack of empathy, a failure to understand that it was his actions that had deprived a man of his life and a family of its husband and father. Two young boys would grow up never knowing their father thanks to Spracklin's fanatical determination to enforce a provincial regulation. But in his mind he was the victim; it was his tragedy, and he deserved the public's sympathy.

Spracklin's acquittal also served a broader political purpose, distracting the public from the actions of his special constables. Any motion for a judicial inquiry into the conduct of the Hallam brothers and their criminal activities while inspectors was quietly shelved. What might have been a hugely embarrassing investigation for Premier Drury and Attorney General Raney was lost in the controversy arising from the shooting at the Chappell House. But the hero-worship quickly came to an end when the Spracklin period was brought into closer focus. In mid-April, the Public Accounts Committee of the provincial legislature began examining the cost of this ill-fated venture. It turned out that Raney had placed a very expensive car and motor launch at Spracklin's disposal. There were numerous travel vouchers and "incidental expenses" paid out to the Hallam brothers. In all, during its three months of existence, the flying squad had cost the taxpayers $2,000 and only recovered $1,100 in fines. They had proved to be far more expensive and much less effective than the regular inspectors sent to the border.

Not only that, there were the legal bills to be paid. The Liquor Board received the lawyers' accounts totaling $1,000 for the Fleming lawsuit and $3,000 for the defence costs on the manslaughter charge. These were enormous bills in 1920, and quite beyond the financial resources of a Methodist preacher. As the months passed and no bills were paid, Oscar Fleming warned that he was not prepared to wait indefinitely, and that he would file writs of execution on Spracklin's house and possessions if the money was not forthcoming. On July 6, 1921, J.H. Rodd wrote to Raney advising him that Fleming was entirely serious and that a further embarrassment was in the offing. W.S. Dingman of the License Board also wrote to Raney suggesting that the provincial government was bound to stand behind him. "Let it be admitted that Spracklin was impetuous at times," Dingman added with understatement. But for good or ill, the Province was obliged to pick up his expenses, for the Liquor board "believes that balance on the whole is to Spracklin's credit, and respectfully recommends that the damages and costs be paid by the Province." Raney concurred and, as discreetly as possible, the bills were paid.[3]

But a far greater embarrassment was in store when the Ontario Second Divisional Court rendered its decision on April 7, 1921, on the appeal of the verdict against Spracklin for searching Oscar Fleming's yacht. The appellate judges did not content themselves with a simple, dignified ruling against the Reverend. Chief Justice Meredith utterly condemned him:

> The office which the defendant (Spracklin) took, without any kind of experience or training, was one for which he has in this case proved himself entirely unfitted. The proper exercise of the duties of a peace officer require much experience, tact, patience, and knowledge or training, and for a partisan to undertake them must be to court just such things as happened in this case: bringing trouble and loss to the unfitted officer, wrong to others and ill-repute to the administration of the law. If the law is to be respected, and properly enforced, the enforcement of it must never be committed to such persons as the defendant...[4]

Meredith characterized Spracklin and his gun-toting squad boarding and searching a vessel they knew had not broken any laws as a "stage burlesque." His conduct was "altogether stupid and inexcusable."

Having dealt with Spracklin, the appeal court went on to administer a written thrashing to the attorney general. Chief Justice Meredith pointed out that the *OTA* was only a provincial creation and that "the provincial legislature has no power to create crimes or to legislate otherwise regarding the criminal law or procedure." Raney's instruction to enforce the *OTA* as if it was on the same level as the *Criminal Code* was simply wrong. And as for the fight against the rum runners, the chief justice reminded the authorities that the statute specifically stated that the provincial temperance law in no way affected liquor transactions with a foreign country. "The object of the Act is to curtail the use in Ontario of intoxicating liquor as a beverage. How could taking liquor out of Ontario thwart that purpose?" asked the chief justice. He continued in a comment that might have been applied to both the attorney general and his inspector, "Anyone, and especially one blinded by zeal, may misunderstand the spirit of an enactment; but no one has any kind of excuse for disregarding its plain words."

Having been thoroughly censured for his brief, embarrassing career in law enforcement, Spracklin seemed to be on the verge of losing his position in the Church. On November 28, 1921, the *Border Cities Star* reported considerable discontent within the congregation at Sandwich Methodist. There were "rumors, charges of negligence in the performance of his church duties by members of the congregation, including several women..." What exactly these rumours entailed, or their relation to female members of the congregation, was not specified. What was known was that there had been a meeting of a faction within the congregation where some "claimed that the 'fighting pastor' had been negligent in his duties to the church." Spracklin denied that there existed any "traitors" among his people and that he intended to stay on in Sandwich.

Barely more than a week later, he was gone. On December 7, 1921, it was announced that the pastor had been given an indefinite leave of absence due to the nerve-wracking experiences he had recently endured. While he remained on the church records as pastor, another minister acted as supply. The Reverend J.O.L. Spracklin would never again preach in Sandwich.[5] Less than a year after his acquittal, Spracklin had not only left the Border Cities, he had left Canada entirely. By 1922, he had a new charge in Cheboygan, Michigan, and thereafter his ministerial life was confined to northeastern Michigan. Perhaps it was more fertile ground for the temperance cause than wet Essex County. In 1931, the Cass City *Chronicle* of northern Michigan reported on the Reverend Spracklin leading a speaking tour through that part of the state on behalf of the Anti-Saloon League.[6] He died in Greenbush, Michigan, in May 1960.

The Trumbles stayed on in Sandwich; they had little choice, for the Chappell House was their only source of income. Lulu continued to operate the roadhouse much as her husband had. She sold liquor and beer without a license while the Sandwich police looked the other way. However, less than a year after Babe's shooting, Lulu was back in court, charged with illegally selling liquor. A drunken group of Detroit customers had instigated a mini-riot on the grounds of the Chappell

The Lido Tavern (formerly the Chappell House) is seen here in 1949.

House. Unable to ignore the situation, the police were obliged to intervene. Still in her mourning clothes, Lulu appeared in Court to answer the charges. They were dismissed when the Detroiters failed to appear.

It could not have been easy for her over the next twenty years to run the roadhouse and raise two boys. But as they got older, Robert and Lester assumed more responsibility, and in 1944, Lulu was able to transfer equal ownership to them. She remarried in the 1940s and died in 1970. By the mid-1940s, the brothers had taken over the operation and had renamed it the Lido-Venice a more refined title that helped to erase the memories of 1920. Together, Robert and Lester ran the roadhouse until they sold out in 1949. A relative remembered that "the Trumble brothers were great men who always put family first and had astonishing morals… Despite the adversity they faced in growing up without a father Les and Robert grew up to be successful, positive and humorous men."[7] As for the roadhouse, by the 1950s it became simply the "Lido Tavern." But after it was sold, it fell on increasingly hard times and became a haven for biker gangs. In 1977, the building was badly damaged by fire and by the 1990s, it was converted into a striptease club. Finally, the structure was completely destroyed by fire in 2006, and the site was razed.

While the shooting of Babe Trumble was quickly buried in the glitz and glam of the 1920s, by the latter half of the twentieth century, it began to assume legendary status. The killing was one of the most significant incidents of the bootlegger era which itself became central to Windsor's self-image. Many families fondly remembered the part their ancestors played in the trade. Artifacts from the era were proudly displayed, and in one of Windsor's major parks, the mast from the rumrunner ship *Vedas* stood watch over playing children. To have been connected to the bootlegging operations was not a shame, and over time it became increasingly a point of honour. Photographs of relatives wearing smuggling gear would proudly be displayed. Numerous area taverns claimed that at one time or another Al Capone had taken a drink in their premises. By the early twenty-first century, groups of performers dressed in 1920s-style took tourists on "rumrunner" tours which invariably included a drive past the Spracklin manse that had been the target of gun fire, as well as the site of the former Chappell House.

As for the confrontation in the Chappell House, it too became part of rumrunner lore, a violent but safely distant episode from the border area's past. In this romanticized version of events, inaccuracies were woven into the weave of history. One was the myth that Beverley Trumble and Leslie Spracklin had been enemies since school days and that a "rivalry brewed like a poison between them."[8] This version fed into a story of a bitter conflict that could only be resolved by the inevitable confrontation. Yet, there are only passing references to their school-days rivalry, and between 1907 and 1920 they seemed to have had nothing whatsoever to do with each other. For that matter, as Spracklin testified, he had gone out of his way to avoid contact with Trumble. The shooting on November 6 was, in many ways, an accidental event. Other writers have gone much farther in embellishing the myth and have attempted to portray Spracklin as a Canadian "Eliott Ness," a "gangster's worst nightmare" who together with his hand-picked squad "burst into the roadhouses of Essex County with pistols drawn and fists clenched."[9] Rather, Spracklin and his men (several of whom were gangsters themselves) never put a serious dent into rumrunning, and their cavalier disdain for civil liberties had the unintended effect of diminishing public support for temperance. Unfortunately, the myths that have grown around both men only detract from the reality of their tragic encounter and an understanding of their times.

In retrospect, Raney's administration of justice, which included the appointment of Spracklin and his special squad, which led to the killing of roadhouse proprietor Beverley Trumble, can be viewed as the final flowering of the nineteenth century evangelical movement. The aspirations of generations of temperance preachers had finally been fulfilled and gained the force of law. But many people simply would not conduct themselves according to the mandates of this new order. In that case, a stern, unflinching enforcement of moral uplift was necessary. In that context, the killing on November 6, 1920, fitted perfectly into how William Raney wished Ontario to be governed. Moral reform was for the general benefit of society, and in order to be effective, it had to be imposed by force. Temperance was no longer a life-enhancing philosophy; it had become a matter "of jails and fines, of pains and penalties."[10] Those stubborn individuals who defied moral uplift were outlaws, and they might have to pay with their lives for their defiance.

Yet this morality by government edict would be hard pressed to accommodate itself to the modern world. After the end of the First World War, it was becoming apparent that a large proportion of the public resented being told what they could drink and how they should live. This was especially true in Ontario's growing industrial cities. Notions of personal liberty, of the right of individuals to enjoy their lives as they chose, were overtaking the strictures of Victorian times. Resentment was also building against a government that required a doctor's prescription to get a drink and which used informants or "spotters" to catch those who did not conform. Employing a reckless zealot like Spracklin also helped turn the majority of the public away from laws based on religious teachings. As historian Peter Oliver observed, "In any case prohibition was doomed to failure and the unbending vigour with which Raney administered the OTA probably only hastened the day of its demise... never again could it (moral uplift) claim to represent the dominant spirit of the age."[11]

Concealing a serious heart ailment, W.E. Raney stayed on as leader of the United Farmers after 1923. In 1927, he was appointed a judge of the Supreme Court of Ontario and was generally considered to be an asset to the bench. News reporter Roy Greenaway, who had done so much to romanticize the bootlegging days of 1920, visited Raney in his library in September 1933, a few weeks before his death. While they reminisced about the Spracklin case, a maid appeared with a glass of milk and a jigger of whisky. Embarrassed, Raney explained that it was for his heart. Turning to Greenaway, he asked "Promise never to say a word of this…What would people say if they heard Raney was imbibing this stuff… a secret drinker!"[12]

Only a few years before, such stuff could cost a man his life.

ENDNOTES

Chapter 1: A Temperate Province

1 J.J. Talman and M.A. Garland, "Pioneer Drinking Habits…" in *Aspects of Nineteenth-Century Ontario: Essays Presented to James J. Talman* (Toronto: University of Toronto Press, 1974), 173; and see Fred Landon, *Western Ontario and the American Frontier* (Toronto: Carleton Library Edition, 1967), 134-5; Patrick Shirreff, *A Tour Through North America* (Edinburgh, 1835); on "buckets of whisky" see Jan Noel, *Canada Dry: Temperance Crusades before Confederation* (Toronto: University of Toronto Press, 1995), 13-4.

2 Brian Douglas Tennyson, "Sir William Hearst and the Ontario Temperance Act," *Ontario History* 55:4 (1963), 233; on Judge R.B. Sullivan's comments see *Toronto Patriot* March 10, 1835; *Canada Temperance Act* (Scott Act) 41 Vict. c. 16 (1878); "of all the reformist churches" see F.L. Barron, "The American Origins of the Temperance Movement in Ontario," *Canadian Review of American Studies* 11 (1980), 136.

3 Adam Coombs, "Liberty and Community: The Political Ideas of the Nineteenth-Century Canadian Temperance Movement," *The Graduate History*

185

Review 3, 1 (2011),"by the 1850s, the focus of the movement became increasingly state-centric as it sought to mobilize public opinion to encourage the state to enact restrictive measure on what was termed the 'liquor traffic.'" (p. 11); and see also the quote from Reverend McKay at 1; on free will and alcohol, Mariana Valverde, *Diseases of the Will: Alcohol and the Dilemmas of Freedom* (Cambridge: Cambridge University Press, 1998); and Sharon Anne Cook, *Through Sunshine and Shadow: The Woman's Christian Temperance Union, Evangelicalism, and Reform in Ontario 1874-1930* (Kingston-Montreal: McGill-Queens University Press, 1995); on the 1898 plebiscite, see Craig Heron, *Booze: A Distilled History* (Toronto: Between the Lines, 2003), 172-3

4 Tennyson, "Sir William Hearst" 240; and see editorial from the *Toronto Globe*, "Honor to Hearst and Rowell," September 16, 1916; on Whitney, see Charles W. Humphries, '*Honest Enough to be Bold': The Life and Times of Sir James Pliny Whitney* (Toronto: University of Toronto Press, 1985), 130-3; on temperance in the 1890s, see Graeme Decarie, "Something Old, Something New…" in Donald Swainson, ed. *Oliver Mowat's Ontario* (Toronto: Macmillan, 1972), 154-71; *Ontario Temperance Act*, Statutes of Ontario, c. 50 (1916).

Chapter 2: An Intemperate City

1 *Windsor Evening Record*, "Police of Detroit," September 18, 1916.

2 Walter Griffith, "A Little Bit of Old France Set Down in Sandwich West" in *Radio Sketches...* (Essex County Historical Association, 1963), 73-4; on John Howison's observations, see *Sketches of Upper Canada, Domestic, Local and Characteristics...* (Edinburgh, 1821: Toronto reprint, 1970), 200; on the Jesuit pears, see Guillaume Teasdale, *The French Orchard Country...* (Toronto, Phd. thesis, York University, 2010), 221.

3 On Ford City, see David Roberts, *In the Shadow of Detroit: Gordon M. McGregor, Ford of Canada and Motoropolis* (Detroit: Wayne State University Press, 2006); on Walkerville, see Ronald G. Hoskins, "A Historical Survey of the Town of Walkerville," (M.A. thesis, University of Windsor, 1964); on the Border Cities, see Patrick Brode, *The River and the Land: A History of Windsor to 1900* (Windsor: Biblioasis, 2014).

4 Brandon Dimmel, "South Detroit, Canada: Isolation, Identity and the US-Canada Border, 1914-1918," *Journal of Borderlands Studies*, vol 26 no. 2 (2011), 207; on horse racing in 1914, see *Evening Record*, July 16, 1914.

5 On the ethnic mixture of Windsor, see *Census of Canada*, 1921 (Ottawa: King's Printer, 1922), the Polish and French communities of London, a city 40% larger than Windsor were almost insignificant when compared to Windsor; on the condition of Poles, see *Windsor Evening Record*, "Walkerville to Segregate Poles in its Own District," September 12, 1917.

6 *Amherstberg Echo*, March 5, 1886; on the increase in tavern licenses, see *Evening Record*, "The Town

Council," February 19, 1875; on Windsor men getting drunk in Detroit on Sundays, see *Evening Record*, August 1, 1875; on Reverend Dewar's concerns, *Windsor Herald*, July 11, 1855.

7 *Evening Record*, "North Essex License," May 11, 1905; on Tolmie, see editorial "Liquor Licenses," April 7, 1903, and "Pastor Roasts The Politicians," April 21, 1902; on J.C. Patterson in Parliament, see *House of Commons Debates*, June 8, 1887, 853; on the plebiscite of 1894, see *Evening Record*, editorial "The Plebiscite," January 4, 1894.

8 Craig Heron, "The Boys and Their Booze: Masculinities and Public Drinking in Working-class Hamilton, 1890-1946," *Canadian Historical Review* 86:3, (September, 2005), 425.

9 *Evening Record* editorial, "License Reduction," April 22, 1912; on Arsas Drouillard, see the meeting of the license commissioners in *Evening Record*, "Grant Ford City License," April 25, 1913, and editorial "Keep Ford City Dry," April 26, 1913; on the Rev. S.L. Toll's campaign, see "Windsor's Civic Administration is Scored," August 12, 1912.

10 *Evening Record* "Neighborhood 'Get the Paper Clubs,'" November 14, 1916; and see Dimmel, "South Canada, Detroit," 202-3; on Captain Brooks Baxter, see *Star*, June 17, 1919.

11 *Evening Record* editorial, "Business of Viewing With Alarm," April 2, 1918.

12 Larry D. Engelmann, "A Separate Peace: The Politics of Prohibition Enforcement in Detroit, 1920-1930," *Detroit in Perspective* 1:1, (September 1972), 51-5; on the American temperance movement, see Thomas R.

Pegram, *Battling Demon Rum: The Struggle for a Dry America, 1800-1933* (Chicago: Ivan Dee, 1998); on J.D. Flavelle's comments on Michigan prohibition, see *Evening Record*, "Dry Michigan," November 8, 1916.

Chapter 3: Fighters

1   *Detroit News*, "Spracklin and Trumble, as Boys, Led Rival gangs," November 8, 1920; on the coming of the two families to Windsor, see *Windsor Municipal Directories* 1893-1917.

2   On Willie Spracklin's career, see *Evening Record* "Spracklin Won It," October 15, 1903; "Can't Beat 'Sprack,'" January 13, 1904; "Went limit of 25 Rounds," July 6, 1906; "Prize Fight Barred in Essex County," March 8, 1906; on death, "Spracklin Shot," November 9, 1907; on Mike Ward's death, *Pittsburgh Press*, November 23, 1906; on the Rev. Prescott condemning the track, see "New Race Tracks Under Heavy Attack by Minister," September 25, 1916.

3   Interview with Kathy Rappaport, granddaughter of a former Ford worker, quoted in Rose Keefe, *The Fighting Parson* (Absolute Crime Books, 2014), 11.

4   Neil Semple, *The Lord's Dominion: The History of Canadian Methodism* (Montreal, Kingston: McGill-Queen's University Press, 1996), 66-70; and 358-9; on the Carman-Jackson controversy, see Michael Gauvreau, *Evangelical Century: College and Creed in English Canada from the Great Revival to the Great*

Depression (Montreal-Kingston: McGill-Queen's U.P., 1991), 241-3.

5 *Windsor Evening Record*, "Modern Vices," November 13, 1916.

6 *Evening Record*, "Ford City to have Two Licenses," April 29, 1913; and see "Fr. Beaudoin bent Upon Reduction of Licenses," March 19, 1909.

7 On Rev. McCombe's sermon, see *Evening Record*, "Windsor's Greatest Devil," March 8, 1911; on Rev. Toll, see "Windsor Civic Administration," August 12, 1912; on Spracklin's theological education, see "To Admit Windsor Man to Ministry," June 2, 1916.

8 *Evening Record*, "Bev. Trumble Gets Beating," June 8, 1914; on his various jobs, see *Windsor Municipal Directory* 1903-1914; on Hamilton Trumble's political career on City Council, see "Trumble's Bile Stirred," October 19, 1904; "Civic Slate Adopted," January 8, 1906; "Ald. Trumble Called Liar," May 22, 1906; February 16, 1909; and "He had No Right to Turn on Fire Alarms," October 4, 1910.

9 On liquor violations at the Chappell House, see *Evening Record*, June 23, 1918, and *Amherstburg Echo*, February 19, 1915; on Henry Chappell, see "Old Turfman Passes Away," July 14, 1906; on Spracklin's transfer to Sandwich, see *Evening Record*, September 7, 1918.

10 *Detroit News*, November 6, 1920.

Chapter 4: Enforcing Temperance

1 On the use of medical prescriptions, see *Evening Record*, August 1 and 2, 1918; and editorial "The

Prohibition Farce," January 4, 1919; on Dr. Gardner, "Charged With Violation," January 2, 1919; and "1,244 Liquor Orders," *Border Cities Star*, January 9, 1919; on Stephen Leacock, see *Wet Wit and Dry Humour* (1931).

2 Gerald Hallowell, *Prohibition in Ontario, 1919-1923* (Toronto: Ontario Historical Society, 1972), 18-9.

3 On agrarian Ontario, see Joseph Schull, *Ontario Since 1867* (Toronto: McClelland & Stewart, 1978); and on Border Cities ethnic diversity, see sixth Census of Canada, 1921, Dominion Publishers, Ottawa (1924), 458; on the Methodist fear of foreigners, see Toronto Methodist Conference, comments by Rev. Wesley Dean; *Toronto Globe*, June 12, 1914.

4 Arthur M. Woodford, *This Is Detroit: 1701-2001* (Detroit: Wayne State University Press, 2001), 86; and Brandon Dimmel, "Sabotage, Security, and Border-Crossing Culture: The Detroit River during the First World War, 1914-1918," *Histoire sociale/Social History* 47, 94 (June 2014), 408; on Windsor's population, see *Census of Canada*, 1921 (Ottawa: King's Printer, 1922).

5 *Border Cities Star*, "Hotel Proprietor" August 19, 1919; and "Liquor Ring," July 12, 1919; and "Carload of Liquor," August 18, 1919; on Detroit's compromise with Prohibition, see Engelmann, "A Separate Peace," 54.

6 *Border Cities Star*, "Debate on Referendum," October 17, 1919; on the *Star*'s support for the *OTA*, see editorial "Prohibition," September 22, 1919; Protestant services urging a "yes" vote in support of

the *OTA*, see "Cause Strengthened," September 29, 1919; quote from the *Christian Guardian* as quoted in Hallowell, *Prohibition in Ontario*, 60.

7 See Heron, *Booze*, 236-8; and Hallowell, *Prohibition in Ontario*, 7-8.

8 Richard N. Kottman, "Volstead Violated: Prohibition as a factor in Canadian-American Relations," *Canadian Historical Review* 43:2 (June, 1962), 109; on the 18th Amendment, see Richard F. Hamm, *Shaping the 18th Amendment* (Chapel Hill: University of North Carolina Press, 1995), 241-53

9 Engelman, "The Politics of Prohibition," 71.

10 *Detroit Free Press*, "Border Rum Sleuths," January 23, 1920; on the "just one bottle rule," see *Free Press*, "Windsor Still Nurses Thirst," January 2, 1920.

11 *Border Cities Star*, "Liquor Deals," February 14, 1920; "Border Cellars" January 14; "Heavier Liquor Fines" January 7; on wife paying bootlegger's fine, see "Bootlegger is Fined $400," March 29, 1920.

12 *Border Cities Star*, "Authorities Plan," April 7, 1920; on the Liberty League and Flavelle, see "Mayor Winter Calls Meeting," April 3, 1920; the vaccination issue, "Many Detroiters," March 22, 1920; Dougall Avenue raid, "Big Seizure," March 1, 1920.

13 *Detroit News*, "Officers Seize Boats and Rum," September 5, 1920; on the Macomb County roadhouses, see *Detroit News*, "Drinking Gambling and Bright Lights Along Lake," June 5, 1920.

14 Tyrell, "Utilizing a Border," 21.

15 *Border Cities Star*, editorial "The Limit Reached," May 22, 1920; on the revenue from fines, see "1919 Lean Year

for Convictions," May 14, 1920, Windsor Magistrate Courts had collected $21,088 for liquor offences in 1919, in one week in May 1920, the same court collected over $18,000 in *OTA* fines; Magistrate Miers comments in *Star*, "Authorities Plan," April 7, 1920; on the Liberty League committee meeting the provincial government, see "Mayor Winter," April 3, 1920, and "Authorities Plan," April 7; on Isadore Katzman's conviction, see "Liquor Stolen," April 21, 1920.

Chapter 5: A Leader Found

1 *Toronto Star* "Dens of Iniquity," July 26, 1920.

2 On Sandwich Methodist Church, see "Service In Sandwich," May 9, 1907; on the Chappell House's activities, see Spracklin's observations in *Star*, June 22, 1920.

3 Comments of Wayne B. Wheeler of the Anti-saloon League, *Detroit Free Press* "500,000 Drive" January 11, 1920.

4 *Border Cities Star* editorial "Enforce the law," May 29, 1920.

5 *Saturday Night* April 19, 1919.

6 *Border Cities Star* editorial "Courageous Action," June 23, 1920; on Donnelly's resentment of outside interference see *Star* June 24, 1920; and "Mayor Donnelly Says Doesn't Think There is Much to Investigate," *Star* June 25, 1920; on the Sandwich Town Council Meeting of June 21, 1920, see Windsor Municipal Archives, R.G. 5, D-1/22, Minutes of the town council, June 21, 1920, 512.

7   On the Amherstburg battle, see *Star* "Bullets Fly," June 28, 1920; and *Amherstburg Echo* "Rum Runners and Boot Leggers Free-For-All," July 2, 1920.

8   *Border Cities Star* "Spracklin Hits Hard," June 28, 1920; on the attack on the Tourangeau farm, see "Sandwich West House is Riddled By Bullets," July 31, 1920.

9   On Walkerville police, see *Border Cities Star* July 14, 1920; on Flavelle's comments "Border Police Criticized," July 13, 1920; on the St. Patrick's Day incident, see "Case Dealing," June 11, 1920; on Amherstburg, see "Amherstburg Has No Police Force," July 17, 1920; on Ministers rallying to Spracklin, see "Back War on Bootleggers," July 8, 1920.

10 *Border Cities Star* "Sandwich Council," July 20, 1920; and *Toronto Globe* "Mr. Spracklin Presents," June 20, 1920.

11 *Toronto Evening Telegram* "Border Bootlegging," in *Border Cities Star* July 7, 1920; and see *Christian Guardian* July 7 and July 14, 1920.

12 *Toronto Star* "Dens of iniquity," July 26, 1920; on the editorial in the *Toronto Globe*, see "Mr. Raney Must Act," July 27, 1920.

13 Peter Oliver, "The New Order: W.E. Raney and the Politics of 'Uplift,'" in *Public and Private Persons: The Ontario Political Culture 1914-1934* (Toronto: Clarke Irwin, 1975), 68.

14 *Toronto Evening Telegram* December 14, 1919, as cited in *Oliver* at 72; on the relationship between Raney and Drury, see Charles M. Johnston, *E.C. Drury: Agrarian Idealist*, (Toronto: University of Toronto Press, 1986), 149-50.

15 *Border Cities Star,* July 28, 1920; on Raney's declaration to clean up the border, see *Star* July 10, 1920; on respectable people as rumrunners see *Globe* July 27, 1920.

16 *Border Cities Star* "Reeve Won't Talk," June 28, 1920; on the police committee investigation, see "Committee Puts Stamp of Approval," July 29, 1920; and Toronto *Star* "Sandwich Police Chief Absolved," July 30, 1920.

17 *Border Cities Star* editorial "Criticizing Mr. Spracklin," September 16, 1920; and see *Christian Guardian* "Methodist Ministers and Public Service," August 4, 1920.

18 On Raney's new directions to the police, see *Border Cities Star* "Fighting Pastor," July 28, 1920; on the Erin speech, see "Raney Raps," August 6, 1920.

Chapter 6: Inspector Spracklin

1 *Border Cities Star* "Inspector Spracklin," July 31, 1920.

2 *Toronto Daily Star* "Spracklin To Be Armed," July 27, 1920.

3 Roy Greenaway, *The Newsgame,* (Toronto: Clarke Irwin, 1966), 26-7; on the comparison of Spracklin to the Black Douglas, see *Toronto Daily Star* July 31, 1920.

4 *Toronto Daily Star* "Mercury had Nothing," October 29, 1920; and "Bootleggers Vowed," October 4, 1920; on the quote on Spracklin's "exceptionally fine" officers, see October 28, 1920, all reports from Greenaway.

5 See Greenaway, *The Newsgame* 27; and *Border Cities Star* "Five Shots Are Fired," October 5, 1920.

6 *Toronto Daily Star* "Bare Plot to Destroy," October 25, 1920.

7 *Toronto Evening Telegram* "Windsor Will Be Wicked," July 8, 1920.

8 Philip P. Mason, *Rumrunning and the Roaring Twenties: Prohibition on the Michigan-Ontario Waterway*, (Detroit: Wayne State University Press, 1995), 41.

9 Paul-Mattias Tyrell, "Utilizing a Border as a Local Economic Resource: The Example of the Prohibition-era Detroit-Windsor Borderland," (1920-33) *Comparative American Studies* 13:1-2 (June 2015), 20; on the introduction of the "Gate Bottle" see Hiram Walker Distillery corporate papers, message from "United Traders Limited" one of Walker's surrogate companies to the parent in Walkerville that the long-necked bottle "was vulnerable to breakage and the neck protruded from the sacks in which they were packed." January 5, 1931.

10 *Border Cities Star* on Rocheleau see "Former Essex Official," July 29, 1920; and "Mayor of Amherstburg," August 27, 1920.

11 *Border Cities Star* "Spracklin Rapped," September 29, 1920.

12 The Dodlawn, Sauve and Dominion House cases were all related to the provincial committee investigating the operation of the Ontario Temperance Act by Windsor lawyer Healy on November 3, 1920.

13 *Toronto Globe* "Police Chase," September 16, 1920.

14 *Border Cities Star* "Protests Against Methods," October 22, 1920; on the success of Mousseau's men in seizing $40,000 worth of liquor, see "Action Started," October 10, 1920; on the "carnival of booze" see *Toronto Daily Star* "Bare plot to Destroy," October 25, 1920.

15 *Toronto Globe* editorial "The Scandal On The Border," September 28, 1920; on Miers comments, see *Amherstburg Echo* October 1, 1920, and his explanation to Raney, *Toronto Daily Star* "Windsor Magistrate," October 2, 1920.

16 *Toronto Daily Star* "Bare Plot to Destroy Mr. Spracklin's Boat," October 25, 1920; on Spracklin being cleared of charges, see *Border Cities Star* "License Officers Freed," October 21, 1920.

17 On the affidavits filed by Windsor cab drivers, see *Toronto Globe* "License Officers to be Investigated," October 18, 1920; on J.C. Tolmie, see report on the 1919 provincial election and Tolmie's statement: "In 1914 I stood for the abolition of the bar. Today it is abolished and, I think, abolished for good. I have been asked to take a temperance stand. I shall not do so. I believe that the question of the referendum is up to the people." *Border Cities Star* "Liquor Issue Fails," October 9, 1919.

Chapter 7: "This Man Spracklin Is a Fool"

1 *Border Cities Star* "Protest to Raney," November 15, 1920.
2 Archives of Ontario, *Records of the Special Committee re: Ontario Temperance Act 1921* (Special Committee)

R.G. 49-102, hearing of September 28, 1920, 49-50 and 1.

3   *Ibid.*, November 2, 1920, 45-61.

4   *Ibid.*, November 3, 1920, 169.

5   *Ibid.*, November 3, 1920, 180-1.

6   *Toronto Globe* editorial "The Essex Scandal," November 5, 1920.

Chapter 8: Bloody Madness

1   Spracklin's account of the shooting is taken from the testimony he gave at the inquest. Reported in the *Border Cities Star* November 8, 1920.

2   *Border Cities Star* "Royal Commission," August 5, 1920; on J.H. Rodd, see *Star* "Threatens," November 30, 1908, in which he stopped prize fighting and stated that "Windsor will not be made a dumping ground for Detroit pugilist aspirants and their friends." And see obituary, *Windsor Daily Star* April 19, 1945.

3   This account of Lulu's testimony is taken from the account in the *Toronto Globe* "Self-Defence Says Spracklin," November 8, 1920. The *Globe* account of her testimony is more detailed than the rest of the account of the inquest which is from the *Border Cities Star.*

4   See *Peterborough Examiner* "The Sandwich Tragedy," November 19, 1920; *Hamilton Spectator* "The Sandwich Tragedy," November 9, 1920; *Toronto Daily Star* "The Sandwich Verdict," November 10, 1920.

5   *Detroit News* November 8, 1920.

6 *Christian Guardian* "The Real Issue at Sandwich," November 17, 1920; and see *Saturday Night* editorial November 27, 1920; London Methodist Conference in *Border Cities Star* November 9, 1920.

7 *Border Cities Star* "Spracklin Pays Visit," November 8, 1920; on Ayearst as a prohibition advocate, see the protest drawn by him for his comments to the Prohibition Convention: *Toronto Globe* February 25, 1921.

8 *Detroit Times* November 8, 1920.

9 *Border Cities Star* "Spracklin Exonerated," November 9, 1920.

10 Only the Detroit newspaper, the *Times* November 8, 1920, gave a detailed description of Beverley Trumble's funeral.

11 *Border Cities Star* November 18, 1920; on Trumble family and J.H. Rodd, see *Star* November 23, 1920; on the laying of charges, see *Star* November 19, 1920.

12 *Border Cities Star* "Spracklin's Band," November 27, 1920.

13 See *Saturday Night* "Spracklin's Reckless Incapacity," November 20, 1920, 36:4, 1; and "Sanguinary Madness of Prohibitionists," 36:5, 1; *Christian Guardian* "The Real Issue At Sandwich," November 17, 1920.

Chapter 9: Trial: Matters of a "Limited Compass"

1 Archives of Ontario, *Records of the Special Committee...* November 2, 1920, p. 53; on

Spracklin's announced attention to continue his police work after the Trumble shooting, see *Toronto Globe* November 11, 1920.

2 On Abramson's prosecution, see *Border Cities Star* December 17 and 18, 1920; on Raney's article see *Star*, November 29, 1922; on Eastern European clubs and drinking in the Border Cities, see Dan Malleck, *Try to Control Yourself: The Regulation of Public Drinking in Post-Prohibition Ontario, 1927-44* (Vancouver: U.B.C. Press, 2012), 207; on Trumble and his black employees, see Toronto *Evening Telegram* "Enforcing OTA," August 5, 1920.

3 *Fleming* v *Spracklin* (1920), vol. 35 *Canadian Criminal Cases* 40 and 43.

4 Joseph Sedgwick, "Sir William Mulock, P.C., K.C.M.G. A Recollection," *Law Society Gazette* (Sept-Dec 1991), 25:3, 288; and see W.J. Loudon, *Sir William Mulock: A Short Biography* (Toronto: Macmillan, 1932).

5 *Detroit News* February 22, 1921.

6 *Detroit News* February 22, 1921.

7 *Border Cities Star* "Crown Counsel" February 22, 1921; on A. Munro Grier, see *Past Members Database*, Law Society of Upper Canada Archives, 2016; on Spracklin and Brackin, see "Lawyer and Pastor in row," August 13, 1920.

8 *Border Cities Star* "Smith 'Star' Witness," February 23, 1921.

9 *Ibid.*, February 24, 1921.

10 *Toronto Star* editorial "The Spracklin Verdict," February 25, 1921; on the Massey Hall demonstration, see *Toronto Evening Telegram*

February 25, 1921; on the provincial assembly, see *Toronto Globe* February 24, 1921; on Dr. Chown and the Sarnia rally, see *Toronto Daily Star* February 28, 1921.

Chapter 10: Learning to Live with Booze

1 *Toronto Globe* "Tentacles of Rum-runner," March 25, 1921.

2 Accounts of the Dominion Alliance rally in Windsor in *Border Cities Star* "Pussyfoot Denied Hearing," April 12, 1921; and *Toronto Globe* "Windsor Hoots Pussyfoot," April 12, 1921.

3 *Border Cities Star* "Raney Calls Law Opponents Traitors," November 29, 1922.

4 *Detroit Free Press* May 20, 1921; on the "liquor pirates," of Riverside, see *Border Cities Star* November 11, 1921.

5 *Border Cities Star* August 10, 1920; on the *New York Herald* reaction to the Gundy ruling, see Daniel Okrent, *Last Call: The Rise and fall of Prohibition* (Simon and Schuster), 152.

6 On the flow of beer to Detroit resulting from Gundy's decision, see *Star* "Look for Increase in Rum Running," August 11, 1921; "Hints Regulation," August 12, 1920; and "Flow of Beer to American Points Unchecked," August 13, 1921.

7 On the *Detroit News* exposé on Prohibition, see "Law of Jungle Rules," September 8, 1923; on nine-percent beer shipments to Michigan, see *Border Cities Star* "Claim 60,000 Cases Shipped," December 10,

1921; on John C. Lodge's tolerance of blind pigs, see Engelmann, "A Separate Peace," 65.

8 As quoted in Oliver, "Public and Private Persons," 85.

9 *Toronto Evening Telegram* April 9, 1921; on the heckler at the Elora meeting, see *Border Cities Star* June 8, 1923; on A.F. Healy's comments during the election, see *Border Cities Star* June 19, 1923.

10 *Border Cities Star* "Detroit Thirsty Flock to Border," May 30, 1925.

11 *Royal Commission on Customs and Excise*: Interim Report (1928); on the career of James Cooper, see *Border Cities Star* February 10, 1931.

12 Tyrell, "Utilizing a Border…," 18.

Chapter 11: The Parting Glass

1 *Border Cities Star* May 28, 1926; and "Both Hallams Found Guilty," June 16, 1921; on the manslaughter charge against Stanley Hallam, see *Toronto World* "Stanley Hallam Blamed for Death," February 9, 1921; on acquittal, see *Toronto Globe* "Spracklin Aide Freed," March 8, 1921; on Jack Bannon, see Susan Goldenberg, *Snatched!: The Peculiar Kidnapping of Beer Tycoon John Labatt* (Toronto: Dundurn, 2004).

2 On Spracklin in London and Paris, see *Toronto World* March 14, 1921; on the Chatham reception, see *Toronto Globe* "Mr. Spracklin Given Old Home Welcome," April 13, 1921.

3 Archives of Ontario, R.G. 4-32 Attorney General Central Registry Criminal and Civil files, *Fleming v Spracklin* file, 1921: J.H. Rodd to Raney July 6,

1921, and W.S. Dingman to Raney June 23, 1921; on the $500 damages owing to Oscar Fleming, see *Border Cities Star* "Government Foots Bill for Spracklin's Illegal Search," September 1, 1921.

4   *Fleming* v *Spracklin* (1921), vol. 38, Canadian Criminal Cases 99 at 100; and see Archives of Ontario, R.G. 4-32 (supra) Reasons for Judgment Second Divisional Court, April 7, 1921.

5   See *Border Cities Star* "Pastor Will Stay," November 28, 1921; "Pastor On Holiday," December 7, 1921.

6   *Cass City Chronicle* January 16, 1931.

7   Comments from Beverley Trumble's great-grandson, Ryan King; on the criminal charges against Lulu Trumble, see *Border Cities Star* "To Appear In Court Today," August 9, 1921; on the transfers of ownership of the Chappell House, see Essex County Land Registry, lot 28, Plan 40 (the author is grateful to Ms. Lucinda Morris for the title search of this property.)

8   Marty Gervais, *The Rumrunners: A Prohibition Scrapbook* (revised) (Windsor: Biblioasis, 2009). The author alleges that there was a long-standing rivalry between the two men (p. 190), but there is no evidence that supports such a proposition. Moreover, the author indicates on page 196 that on the evening of November 6, Spracklin "raced through the main dining room into the main hall and through to the bar in search of Trumble, but couldn't find him." This is simply inaccurate; as Spracklin stated at the inquest, he was searching for liquor.

9   Rose Keefe, *The Fighting Parson: The Life of Reverend Leslie Spracklin Canada's Eliot Ness* (Absolute Crime, 2014), 6-7.

10 Gerald A. Hallowell, *Prohibition in Ontario*, 167.
11 Peter Oliver, *Public and Private Persons...*, 90.
12 Roy Greenaway, *The Newsgame*, 35.

SELECT BIBLIOGRAPHY

Primary Sources

Archives of Ontario: R.G. 49-102 *Records of the Special Committee on the Temperance Act 1921* R.G. 4-32

Attorney General Central Registry Criminal and Civil Files, *Fleming v. Spracklin*, 1921

Law Society of Upper Canada Archives: files on J.H. Rodd and Sir William Mulock

United Church of Canada Archives: file on Rev. J.O.L. Spracklin

Windsor Municipal Archives: R.G. 8 *Windsor Police Annual Reports* file 3, 1922

Newspapers

Amherstburg Echo
Border Cities Star (Windsor)
Christian Guardian (Toronto)
Detroit Free Press
The Detroit News
Detroit Times
Hamilton Spectator

Peterborough Examiner
Port Hope Evening Guide
Toronto Daily Star
Toronto Evening Telegram
Toronto Globe
Toronto World
Saturday Night (Toronto)
Windsor Evening Record

Books and Articles

Dimmel, Brandon, "South Detroit, Canada Isolation, Identity and the US-Canada Border, 1914-1918" *Journal of Borderlands Studies* 26:2 (2011)

Engelmann, Larry D., "A Separate Peace: The Politics of Prohibition Enforcement in Detroit, 1920-1930" *Detroit In Perspective* I:1 (1972)

Greenaway, Roy, *The Newsgame* (Toronto: Clarke Irwin, 1966)

Keefe, Rose, *The Fighting Parson* (Absolute Crime Books, 2014)

Hallowell, Gerald, *Prohibition in Ontario, 1919-1923* (Toronto: Ontario Historical Society, 1972)

Heron, Craig, *Booze: A Distilled History* (Toronto: Between the Lines, 2003)

Mason, Philip, *Rumrunning and the Roaring Twenties: Prohibition on the Michigan-Ontario Waterway* (Detroit: Wayne State University Press, 1995)

Oliver, Peter, *Public and Private Persons: The Ontario Political Culture 1914-1934* (Toronto: Clarke Irwin, 1975)

Tyrell, Paul-Mattias, "Utilizing a Border as a

Local Economic Resource: The Example of the Prohibition-era Detroit-Windsor borderland (1920-33)" *Comparative American Studies* vol. 13 no. 1-2 (2015)

Valverde, Mariana, *Diseases of the Will: Alcohol and the Dilemmas of Freedom* (Cambridge: Cambridge University Press, 1998)

Woodford, Arthur, *This is Detroit: 1701-2001* (Detroit: Wayne State University Press, 2001)

INDEX

Patrick Brode was born in Windsor, Ontario. He was called to the Ontario Bar in 1977 and has practiced law ever since. He has written five works on the history of law in Canada including *Sir John Beverley Robinson: Bone and Sinew of the Compact*, which was a finalist for the City of Toronto Book Award in 1985, and *The Odyssey of John Anderson*, a finalist for the Trillium Award in 1990. His book *The Slasher Killings: A Canadian Sex-Crime Panic, 1945-1946* was nominated for the 2009 Arthur Ellis Award. His most recent book *Border Cities Powerhouse: The Rise of Windsor: 1900–1945* was shortlisted for the 2017 Ontario Speaker's Book Award.